Devil's Advocates

DEVIL'S ADVOCATES is a series of books devoted to exploring the classics of horror cinema. Contributors to the series come from the fields of teaching, academia, journalism and fiction, but all have one thing in common: a passion for the horror film and a desire to share it with the widest possible audience.

'The admirable Devil's Advocates series is not only essential – and fun – reading for the serious horror fan but should be set texts on any genre course.'
Dr Ian Hunter, Reader in Film Studies, De Montfort University, Leicester

'Auteur Publishing's new Devil's Advocates critiques on individual titles… offer bracingly fresh perspectives from passionate writers. The series will perfectly complement the BFI archive volumes.' **Christopher Fowler,** *Independent on Sunday*

'Devil's Advocates has proven itself more than capable of producing impassioned, intelligent analyses of genre cinema… quickly becoming the go-to guys for intelligent, easily digestible film criticism.' *Horror Talk.com*

'Auteur Publishing continue the good work of giving serious critical attention to significant horror films.' *Black Static*

 DevilsAdvocatesbooks

DevilsAdBooks

ALSO AVAILABLE IN THIS SERIES

A Girl Walks Home Alone at Night Farshid Kazemi
Black Sunday Martyn Conterio
The Blair Witch Project Peter Turner
Blood and Black Lace Roberto Curti
The Blood on Satan's Claw David Evans-Powell
Candyman Jon Towlson
Cannibal Holocaust Calum Waddell
Cape Fear Rob Daniel
Carrie Neil Mitchell
The Company of Wolves James Gracey
The Conjuring Kevin J. Wetmore Jr.
Creepshow Simon Brown
Cruising Eugenio Ercolani & Marcus Stiglegger
The Curse of Frankenstein Marcus K. Harmes
Daughters of Darkness Kat Ellinger
Dawn of the Dead Jon Towlson
Dead of Night Jez Conolly & David Bates
The Descent James Marriot
The Devils Darren Arnold
Don't Look Now Jessica Gildersleeve
The Evil Dead Lloyd Haynes
The Fly Emma Westwood
Frenzy Ian Cooper
Halloween Murray Leeder
House of Usher Evert Jan van Leeuwen
In the Mouth of Madness Michael Blyth

It Follows Joshua Grimm
Ju-on The Grudge Marisa Hayes
Let the Right One In Anne Billson
M Samm Deighan
Macbeth Rebekah Owens
The Mummy Doris V. Sutherland
Nosferatu Cristina Massaccesi
The Omen Adrian Schober
Peeping Tom Kiri Bloom Walden
Possession Alison Taylor
Re-Animator Eddie Falvey
Repulsion Jeremy Carr
Saw Benjamin Poole
Scream Steven West
The Shining Laura Mee
Shivers Luke Aspell
The Silence of the Lambs Barry Forshaw
Suspiria Alexandra Heller-Nicholas
The Texas Chain Saw Massacre James Rose
The Thing Jez Conolly
Trouble Every Day Kate Robertson
Twin Peaks: Fire Walk With Me Lindsay Hallam
Witchfinder General Ian Cooper

FORTHCOMING

Pet Sematary Shellie McMurdo
Poltergeist Rob McLaughlin
Snuff Mark McKenna

Devil's Advocates

IT Chapters One and Two

Alissa Burger

Acknowledgments

Writing a book can often be a lonely business, but much like the Losers, I couldn't do it alone.

Librarians have always been allies and friends in my writing and research, and this book was no different. Robyn Lambert (Culver-Stockton College) was particularly wonderful in helping me track down hard-to-find sources.

The teams from Devil's Advocates and Liverpool University Press have been great to work with, especially John Atkinson and the peer reviewers, who provided thoughtful and encouraging feedback.

I am immensely grateful to Sally Kintz, who formatted all of the images.

Matt and Paige were the best movie dates anyone could ask for for *IT Chapter Two*.

And a big shout-out to the Losers Club of Halloween 2019: Caylee, Courtney, Kaity, Krista, and Remy.

First published in 2023 by
Auteur, an imprint of
Liverpool University Press,
4 Cambridge Street,
Liverpool
L69 7ZU

This paperback edition published 2025

Series design: Nikki Hamlett at Cassels Design
Set by Carnegie Book Production, Lancaster

All rights reserved. No part of this publication may be reproduced in any material form (including photocopying or storing in any medium by electronic means and whether or not transiently or incidentally to some other use of this publication) without the permission of the copyright owner.

All illustrations from *IT Chapter One* and *IT Chapter Two* © New Line Cinema / RatPac-Dune Entertainment / Vertigo Entertainment

British Library Cataloguing-in-Publication Data
A catalogue record for this book is available from the British Library

ISBN hardback: 978-1-802-07715-5
ISBN paperback: 978-1-83624-402-8
ISBN PDF: 978-1-802-07897-8

Contents

Figures vii

Introduction 1

Chapter 1: Text, Time, and Adaptation 11

Chapter 2: Coming Home to Horror 23

Chapter 3: Pennywise the Dancing Clown 43

Chapter 4: Adolescence, Abjection, and Fear 69

Chapter 5: The Return of the Repressed 93

Conclusion 113

Bibliography 117

Figures

Figure 1. King's cameo as a shopkeeper in *IT Chapter Two* 14

Figure 2. Downtown Derry 23

Figure 3. Navigating Derry's history 31

Figure 4. Synthesizing past and present in the Losers' reflection 35

Figure 5: Mr Keene's Pennywise-ish leer 36

Figure 6. The inversion of the funhouse tunnel 50

Figure 7. Pennywise's costuming and physicality 54

Figure 8. Putting on It's Pennywise face 59

Figure 9. Tilted Stan 81

Figure 10. Bev and the idealizing male gaze 86

Figure 11. The Losers in the Barrens 93

Figure 12. The reunited Losers 95

Introduction

2017 was a banner year for the horror genre, with films like Jordan Peele's *Get Out* and M. Night Shyamalan's *Split* earning not just big box office returns but critical attention as well. *Get Out* scored multiple Academy Award nominations, including Best Picture, Best Director (Jordan Peele), and Best Actor (Daniel Kaluuya), as well as Best Original Screenplay, which Peele won. This kind of critical acclaim is nearly unheard of for horror films: prior to the success of *Get Out*, the only horror films to have been nominated for Best Picture were *Rebecca* (1940), *The Exorcist* (1973), *Jaws* (1975), *Silence of the Lambs* (1991), and *The Sixth Sense* (1999), though some of these films side-stepped the horror designation, with *Rebecca* described as suspense and *Silence of the Lambs* largely marketed as a thriller, despite the overtly horrific elements in both films, which range from the Gothic to the grotesque. The tenor of conversations surrounding horror changed as well, garnering more serious attention from reviewers and general audiences, with *Vanity Fair*'s Laura Bradley penning an article on the 2010s as "[T]he Decade Horror Got 'Elevated,'"[1] though the notion of "elevated horror" is itself a contested one.[2]

Established horror franchises earned big bucks at the box office as well, including *Annabelle: Creation*, which made more than $100 million and edged the *Conjuring* franchise over the one-billion-dollar mark.[3] Other notable horror series with new releases in 2017 included *Alien: Covenant*, *Amityville: The Awakening*, and a return to the *Saw* universe with *Jigsaw*. Add to this standalone films like Darren Aronofsky's *Mother!*, the indie film *It Comes at Night*, the folk horror of *The Ritual*, and the slasher-style *Happy Death Day*, and horror fans had plenty to choose from when looking for scary good fun.

However, it was Andy Muschietti's *IT Chapter One*[4] that was the big record-breaker of 2017. Anticipation for the film was high and "The trailer set a new record for most views in a twenty-four hour period."[5] On September 8, 2017, the film debuted with a $123 million opening, the highest-grossing preview total for any R-rated film, a total U.S. gross of more than $327 million, and over $700 million worldwide.[6] Muschietti's film is based on the epic novel *IT* by Stephen King, who is no stranger to Hollywood adaptation of his work, which has run the gamut from remarkable (*Misery* [1990], *The Shawshank Redemption* [1994], *The Green Mile* [1999]) to awful (*The Lawnmower*

Man [1992], countless *Children of the Corn* sequels). In addition to *IT Chapter One*, King adaptations abounded in 2017, with the long-anticipated (and largely panned) film *The Dark Tower*; television series *The Mist* (Spike), and *Mr. Mercedes* (Audience); and two Netflix original films, *Gerald's Game* and *1922*.

What made 2017 the year of the horror film? First and foremost is the central role horror has always played in reflecting and negotiating both perennial horrors and the fears of its current moment. Homing in on this interconnection, Barry Keith Grant makes the argument:

> Horror movies exploit timeless themes of sex and death, the self and the soul, and our own beastly inner nature—fears that exist within our collective unconscious—as well as more topical fears such as, for example, atomic radiation in the 1950s, environmental contamination in the 1970s and 1980s, or more recently, post-9/11 tourist horror with films such as *Touristas* (2006), *The Ruins* (2008), and the two *Hostel* films (2005, 2007).[7]

The latter half of the 2010s were years of great social and political unrest in the United States and across the world. Haleigh Foutch notes the horrors of 2017 specifically, which she argued "has by and large been one of the most traumatic, discordant years in American history, from politics and renewed threats of nuclear war, to natural disasters and acts of domestic terrorism."[8] *Forbes*'s Rob Cain notes that this spike of horror coincides with earlier trends, explaining: "It's notable that the last time horror enjoyed such heights of popularity was also a period of heightened fear and unrest in America,"[9] with 1999–2002 providing *The Sixth Sense*, *The Blair Witch Project* (1999), the final film in the original *Scream* trilogy (2000), the zombie film *28 Days Later* (2002), and *The Ring* (2002; the U.S. remake of the 1998 Japanese horror film *Ringu*), alongside real-world turmoil like the impeachment trial of Bill Clinton, 9/11, and the Iraq War. Similarly, in 2017 with so many real-world threats of danger, violence, and the abuse of power, the cathartic experience of sitting in a darkened theater, popcorn in hand, and screaming at fictional on-screen horrors was a welcome release.

This particular historical and cultural context may also provide clues to the shift in conversations surrounding horror films, as viewers who did not traditionally consider themselves horror fans were drawn into the darkness. Horror Writers Association president John Palisano argued in 2017 that "Horror is speaking to all generations in a way it never has before."[10] As a result, horror films got intensified mainstream media attention and this—coupled with a slate of diverse, high-quality films, including a few high-profile record-breakers like *Get Out* and *IT Chapter One*—resulted in the zeitgeisty conversation surrounding so-called "elevated" horror. However, it is not horror itself that has changed, but rather the audience and the cultural moment, which has drawn these fears—both internal and external, the eternal and the timely—into sharp relief. As Bradley argues, "maybe it's not horror that got elevated, but that this has become the decade when mainstream audiences finally started to notice."[11] One of the 2017 horror films of which audiences took the most notice was Muschietti's *IT Chapter One*.

IT's development and path to the big screen was a complicated and protracted one. The project was initially announced in 2009, with Dave Kajganich (*The Invasion* [2007], *Suspira* [2018]) hired to write the script. In this early iteration, *IT* was planned as a single feature film, set in the present day.[12] In 2012, the studio shifted its approach, bringing on Cary Fukunaga (*Sin Nombre* [2009], *Jane Eyre* [2011], *True Detective* [2014]), who was slated to direct *IT* as two films, co-writing the script with Chase Palmer.[13] However, this version also failed to come to fruition, with Fukunaga claiming artistic differences between himself and studio executives and leaving the project in 2015.[14] Shortly after Fukunaga's departure, Andy Muschietti came on to the project as director, with *IT* again being developed as a two-film project. Gary Dauberman joined the film as a screenwriter, though Fukunaga and Chase also retain screenwriting credit for *IT Chapter One* for their earlier contributions; Dauberman has solo screenwriting credit for *IT Chapter Two*. Casting was announced in mid-2016 for the first film, including the selection of actors to portray the young Losers, though the most buzzworthy casting announcement was the selection of Bill Skarsgård to play Pennywise.[15]

IT Chapter One was filmed on location in and around Port Hope, Ontario and Riverdale, Toronto, with additional filming done at Pinewood Toronto Studios and production running from June 27 to September 21, 2016.[16] *IT Chapter One* opened in more than 4,100 theaters on September 8, 2017 and began its record-breaking run.[17] *IT Chapter Two* returned to the same locations for filming from July 2 to October 30, 2018,[18] with the second film released on September 6, 2019 in more than

4,500 theaters.[19] *IT Chapter Two* did not achieve the record-breaking numbers of its predecessor but, according to *Box Office Mojo*, the film still posted a more than $91 million opening, $211 million total U.S. gross, and $473 million worldwide.[20]

In addition to the record-breaking box office performance of *IT Chapter One*, Pennywise and the Losers went on to become a popular culture phenomenon as well, with an amount of memes and merchandising usually reserved for horror films that are either classics or part of an already-established and successful franchise. From Halloween costumes, clothing, and accessories to games, puzzles, and a wide range of collectibles, Pennywise was ubiquitous as the decade neared its close. There was a Neibolt Street Haunted House Experience in Hollywood prior to the release of *IT Chapter One*,[21] a Neibolt Street virtual reality experience launched to coincide with the release of *IT Chapter One* on blu-ray and DVD, and a Derry Canal Days Festival and Funhouse in Hollywood leading up to the release of *IT Chapter Two*[22] for fans who wanted to immerse themselves in *IT*'s world.

This popular culture obsession with all things *IT* reflects the ways in which Muschietti's two films and the narrative on which they build occupy a unique place within the horror landscape. Like iconic ongoing franchises such as *Halloween* and *Friday the 13th*, Muschietti's *IT* films allow viewers to return to a recognizable narrative pattern and a familiar, nostalgically remembered villain. Well-known and expected scares—from both the classic horror tropes that informed King's novel and the unforgettable images from Tommy Lee Wallace's 1990 miniseries—are coupled with new terrors, providing a modern perspective on an old story, in an updated time frame and with fresh faces. As a narrative of repression, remembering, and returning, the story of *IT* is both timeless and timely and, as Muschietti's films show, It always comes back.

Chapter 1, "Text, Time, and Adaptation," frames *IT Chapter One* and *Chapter Two* within the larger context of King's canon and addresses critical considerations of the adaptation process, remakes, and sequels. Chapter 2, "Coming Home to Horror," explores Derry itself, with a particular focus on Derry's liminality and its position as a traditionally Gothic "Bad Place" where the past and present are inextricably intertwined. Chapter 3, "Pennywise the Dancing Clown," examines the horrific history of clowns, with a close reading of Pennywise's physicality, costuming, and makeup within the context of this larger tradition. The next two chapters provide close readings of the Losers: Chapter 4, "Adolescence, Abjection, and Fear," considers the Losers' childhood encounters with It, including Muschietti's negotiation of each character's experience of abjection through the externalization of their internalized horror. Chapter 5, "The Return of the Repressed," focuses on the adult Losers' return to Derry, the synthesis of their experiences as children and as adults, and the shift from restorative to deconstructive nostalgia in *IT Chapter Two*, which creates a singular, cohesive, and complex narrative across both films of horror, friendship, and the complicated nature of both individual and collective memory.

SYNOPSIS

IT Chapter One opens on a rainy afternoon in October 1988, as Bill Denbrough (Jaeden Martell, previously credited as Jaeden Lieberher) makes a paper boat for his younger brother Georgie (Jackson Robert Scott). Georgie chases his boat through the flooded streets until it is lost down a storm drain, where Georgie is killed and taken by Pennywise the Dancing Clown (Bill Skarsgård).

Jumping forward to June 1989, Bill and his friends Eddie Kaspbrak (Jack Dylan Grazer), Richie Tozier (Finn Wolfhard), and Stan Uris (Wyatt Oleff) are looking forward to the summer to come, though they are reminded of the dangers of Derry through the town curfew, posters of missing kids, and their confrontations with the local bullies, including Henry Bowers (Nicholas Hamilton). Ben Hanscom (Jeremy Ray Taylor) also lives in terror of Bowers, while Beverly Marsh (Sophia Lillis) is attacked by Gretta (Megan Charpentier) and her gang of mean girls (Kasie Rayner and Isabelle Nélisse).

Drawn together as the summer begins, the self-proclaimed Losers Club have fun riding bikes and swimming in the quarry, while also finding themselves drawn more deeply into the horrors of Derry, from the dark history Ben has researched to each individual's encounter with the many permutations of It, as Eddie sees a leper, Bill encounters an undead version of his brother, and Bev's bathroom sink explodes in a geyser of blood. They compare notes, dig deeper into the mystery of the missing kids, and save Mike Hanlon (Chosen Jacobs) from Bowers and his friends (Jake Sim and Logan Thompson), with Mike becoming the final member of the Losers Club.

The Losers track Pennywise to an abandoned house on Neibolt Street, where they encounter additional horrors and come face-to-face with Pennywise,[23] injuring the monster before It retreats once more to the sewer. After this near-death experience, the Losers Club is splintered, though they come back together to fight when Pennywise takes Bev. Bill, Eddie, Richie, Stan, Ben, and Mike descend into the sewers beneath Derry and discover Pennywise's lair, where Bev is held under the power of Pennywise's "deadlights," though Ben is able to wake her with a fairy-tale kiss. Though Pennywise offers the rest of the Losers Club a chance to leave by sacrificing Bill, they refuse and collectively fight It, which transforms to showcase a wide range of It's different faces as it fights each Loser in turn. They once again hurt It, though they are unable to destroy the monster, which retreats to a deeper level of the sewer. In the Barrens, as summer ends, the Losers make a promise to come back and fight if It ever returns.

IT Chapter Two picks up the lives of the Losers 27 years later, when the monster's cycle has come around again, briefly showcasing their adult lives before they are called once more back to Derry, with the exception of Stan (Andy Bean), who commits suicide. When they receive Mike's (Isaiah Mustafa) phone call, telling them they need to return to Derry, each realizes how little of their childhoods they remember. As they are reunited and begin walking Derry's familiar streets once more, their memories begin to return. Mike provides a metaphysical explanation for It, as an extraterrestrial Other that crash-landed in Derry millions of years ago, and details a Native American ritual (the Ritual of Chüd) for defeating It. In addition to It, the Losers are also pursued by enemies both mortal and supernatural, including an adult Henry Bowers (Teach Grant) and the undead Patrick Hockstetter (Owen Teague), who serves as Bowers' chauffer.

IT Chapter Two is fragmented in two key ways. First, there is the distinction of the Losers together and the Losers alone. While their greatest power as children was—and as adults, continues to be—in solidarity with one another, they find themselves separated, both in their own lives before remembering Derry and once they have returned, on their own again as they search for the tokens that they need for the Ritual of Chüd that Mike is confident will defeat It once and for all. In addition, the film also shifts back and forth between the Losers' childhoods and adulthoods, foregrounding a range of flashbacks that fill in narrative blanks from the first film, moments when the Losers were separated from one another in the summer of 1989.

After Pennywise takes a child right in front of Bill (James McAvoy), taunting Bill with his inability to save this boy just as he failed to save his brother Georgie, Bill returns to the house on Neibolt Street, determined to stop Pennywise on his own, once and for all. However, before Bill can enter the house, he is joined by the rest of the Losers Club. After being terrorized by various permutations of It within the house, including as a monstrous spider made of young Stan's severed head, the Losers descend into the sewers below Derry once more. They rediscover Pennywise's lair from their childhood confrontation, and this time descend even further, to where It originally landed. After the Ritual of Chüd fails, the Losers are once again separated to encounter some of their own worst fears—such as Bill facing Georgie and his childhood self in his flooded basement and Beverly (Jessica Chastain) once more trapped in the school bathroom stall—before a final collective confrontation with It. Following the ritual's adage that "All living things must abide by the laws of the shape they inhabit" (*IT Chapter Two*), the Losers attempt to bring It physically down to size and, when that fails, emotionally and psychologically denigrate the monster, minimizing it as a "clown" and a "mimic" (*IT Chapter Two*) with no power over them, before removing and crushing It's heart, though Richie (Bill Hader) is briefly caught in It's deadlights and Eddie (James Ransone) dies in the attempt. Despite these terrible losses, the monster is defeated and the Losers go back to their adult lives, this time with their memories intact.

Notes

1. Laura Bradley, "This Was the Decade Horror Got 'Elevated,'" *Vanity Fair*, 17 Dec. 2019, https://www.vanityfair.com/hollywood/2019/12/rise-of-elevated-horror-decade-2010s.
2. David Church, author of *Post-Horror: Art, Genre, and Cultural Elevation* (2021) uses the terms "post-horror" and "elevated horror" interchangeably to describe "a new wave of films combining horror tropes with the slow pace, austere style, serious themes, and narrative ambiguity found in minimalist art films. They tend to downplay reassuringly familiar clichés and instead display a lot more stylistic restraint, forcing audiences to soak in uncomfortable moods like angst and dread" (qtd. in Helena Heald, "What is Post-Horror? A Q&A with David Church, author of *Post-Horror: Art, Genre, and Cultural Elevation*," *Edinburgh University Press*, 29 Oct. 2021). While some critics have argued that these "elevated horror" films demonstrate more subtlety and "smartness" than their traditional counterparts and are less heavily reliant on jump scares or gore (Tom Nicholson, "The

2010s Were The Decade When Horror Got Smart," *Esquire*, 20 Dec. 2019, https://www.esquire.com/uk/culture/film/a30284121/elevated-horror-2010s-peele-eggers-aster-blumhouse/), this notion enforces a problematic high vs. low culture dichotomy and dismisses the innovative and artistic work being done within the genre for decades, though ignored by the so-called "mainstream" audience. Since its inception, horror has been a marginalized and denigrated genre and the tenor of the "elevated horror" conversation, Jake Harris argues, is that "the 'elevated horror' genre includes horror films that a highbrow audience feels like they could get away with consuming, instead of 'slumming it' with a genre film ... It's better looking and has more depth than those slasher films, so it's not 'really' horror" (Jake Harris, "There's No Such Thing as an 'Elevated Horror' Movie," *Book and Film Globe*, 7 Oct. 2020, https://www.bookandfilmglobe.com/film/theres-no-such-thing-as-an-elevated-horror-movie/.). While this communicates a sense of prestige to potential viewers, as well as directors and actors who might otherwise turn down the project in question, it also overlooks and discounts the sophisticated, meta-textual and culturally engaged work of decades of horror films that have come before. "Elevated horror" is also sometimes referred to as "social horror" with a reputation for addressing issues like racism, sexism, and traditional power structures, with *Esquire*'s Tom Nicholson noting the 2010s as a decade in which "directors reflected a society in turmoil in ways that had never been done before." However, this claim belies a fundamental lack of familiarity with the genre and its historical tradition, as horror has been tackling these issues effectively and inventively since its inception. As Jacob Knight writes (Jacob Knight, "There's No Such Thing as an 'Elevated Horror Movie' (And Yes, 'Hereditary' is a Horror Movie)," *Slash Film*, 8 June 2018, https://www.slashfilm.com/elevated-horror/):

> A heavy influence on *Get Out*, *Night of the Living Dead* cast a black man as the lead, and then used his character to comment upon the age's ingrained racism ... *The Texas Chain Saw Massacre* and *Last House On the Left* saw their architects – Tobe Hooper and Wes Craven, respectively – using handheld cameras to transmute images transmitted from Vietnam into drive-in and 42nd Street screams of defiance. John Carpenter's *Halloween* let us know that evil could invade even the whitest '*safe space*': suburbia. (original emphasis)

"Elevated horror" is a buzzword and a marketing phrase but, in terms of the content of the films themselves, has very little meaning, particularly when it comes to quality. The term is an act of erasure that problematically ignores the wealth of films that have come before, the impact and influence of these films, and the viewers who have watched, loved, and championed them.

3. Haleigh Foutch, "How 2017 Became a Landmark Year for Horror Movies," *Collider*, 21 Dec. 2017, https://www.collider.com/horror-movies-2017-box-office-records/.

4. Initially marketed as simply *IT*, this is revised to *IT Chapter One* in the title that precedes the film's closing credits, in expectation of *Chapter Two* and establishing the film's position as part of a larger narrative.
5. Alyse Wax, *The World of IT* (New York: Abrams, 2019), 12.
6. Jeremy Fuster, "'It' Has Broken a Box Office Record Every Day for the Past Week," *The Wrap*, 15 Sept. 2017, https://www.thewrap.com/it-box-office-record/; "It," *Box Office Mojo*, n.d., https://www.boxofficemojo.com/release/rl3481241089/.
7. Barry Keith Grant, "Screams on Screen: Paradigms of Horror," *Thinking After Dark* (Special Issue: Welcome to the World of Horror Video Games), vol. 4, no. 6 (2010), 4.
8. Foutch.
9. Rob Cain, "2017 Is the Biggest Year for Horror in Decades," *Forbes*, 16 Oct. 2017, https://www.forbes.com/sites/robcain/2017/10/16/2017-is-the-biggest-year-for-horror-in-decades/?sh=5f2ebcb652d9.
10. Quoted in Bradley.
11. Bradley.
12. Ben Child, "It's coming, as Hollywood plans Stephen King Adaptation," *The Guardian*, 13 Mar. 2009, https://www.theguardian.com/film/2009/mar/13/stephen-king-it-film-adaptation; Owen Williams, "Stephen King's It – Everything You Need to Know," *Empire Online*, 11 Aug. 2016, https://www.empireonline.com/movies/features/stephen-king-everything-need-know/.
13. Sandy Schaefer, "Stephen King's 'It' Getting Two-Film Adaptation by 'Jane Eyre' Director," *Screen Rant*, 8 June 2012, https://www.screenrant.com/stephen-king-it-movies-cary-fukunaga/; Williams.
14. Russ Fischer, "Cary Fukunaga Explains the Demise of His Unconventional 'IT' Adaptation," *Slash Film*, 3 Sept. 2015, https://www.slashfilm.com/cary-fukunaga-it/ #more-312794.
15. The role of Pennywise had previously been cast with Will Poulter (*The Maze Runner* [2014], *Midsommar* [2019]) in Fukunaga's earlier conception of the film (Williams).
16. Ra Moon, "Where Was It Filmed? Stephen King's It Chapter 1 & 2 Filming Locations," *Atlas of Wonders*, 2020, https://www.atlasofwonders.com/2017/09/it-filming-locations.html.
17. Wax, 12.
18. Wax, 12.
19. "It Chapter Two," *Box Office Mojo*, n.d., https://www.boxofficemojo.com/release/rl1107461633/.
20. "It Chapter Two," *Box Office Mojo*.

21. Steve Biodrowski, "Haunted House Review: The IT Experience," *Hollywood Gothique*, 9 Sept. 2017, http://www.new.hollywoodgothique.com/haunted-house-review-the-it-experience/.
22. Steve Biodrowski, "Festival & Funhouse Review: The IT Experience Chapter Two," *Hollywood Gothique*, 23 Aug. 2019, http://www.new.hollywoodgothique.com/it-experience-two-review/.
23. In describing It's Pennywise persona, I employ he/him pronouns, as this iteration of the monster is defined as predominantly masculine, and he/him pronouns are regularly used for Pennywise by both the fandom and scholars writing about *IT*. In referring to It's larger identity, including It's disembodied presence, influence, and predation, I use the third person singular pronouns "it" and "its." "It's" is used for the possessive form of the proper noun "It" when referring to the monster itself.

Chapter 1: Text, Time, and Adaptation

While Muschietti's films may have been the first time some viewers made the acquaintance of Pennywise the Dancing Clown, *IT Chapter One* and *Chapter Two* come with a lot of previously established critical engagements and expectations for many viewers, including as an adaptation of King's 1986 novel, as part of King's larger body of work in both literature and popular culture, and as a remake of Tommy Lee Wallace's 1990 television miniseries, including Tim Curry's iconic performance as Pennywise the Dancing Clown.

King noted of the writing of *IT*: "The book is the summation of everything I have done and learned in my whole life to this point … Every monster that ever lived is in this book. This is it, this is the final exam."[1] While King's novels up to this point in his career had included a range of terrifying monsters, both human and supernatural, with *IT* he includes them all: a mummy, a leper, a Rodan-esque giant bird, and, of course, a terrifying clown, among a host of others. This mammoth book—1,138 pages in the hardcover first edition—spans decades, multiple perspectives, and a range of horrors from fairy-tale monsters to cosmic terror. Structurally, King's novel alternates between the past and the present, from the 1957 death of Georgie Denbrough, the cycle of missing and murdered children it kicks off, and the Losers' 1958 summer to their return to Derry in 1985, 27 years later. While this division between time periods is initially distinct and clearly demarcated by separate chapters and sections, as the novel progresses, the lines between past and present blur, with King transitioning from one chapter subsection to the next in mid-sentence, drawing the two times inexorably together as each informs and engages with the other, an approach to structure and transition that Muschietti embraces in *IT Chapter Two*. Using an omniscient narrative perspective, King provides readers with the points of view of each member of the Losers Club, some of their notable adversaries (like Henry Bowers), and a wide-angle historical context of the history of Derry, featured in the novel's "interlude" sections.

While *IT* is one of King's most well-known and popular novels, it is not without its criticism. The most controversial scene in the novel features the male Losers, who have become helplessly lost in the sewers beneath Derry following their childhood showdown with It, each having sex with Beverly, as a way of bringing them all together and, through that solidarity, finding their way back to the world above. The violent anti-gay attack on Adrian Mellon (inspired by the real-life murder of Charlie Howard in Bangor in 1984) that introduces It's reawakening is brutal. Bill Denbrough's final showdown with It through the Ritual of Chüd is esoteric and cosmically informed, an internal battle of the wills that transports Bill to the very edge of the universe in a search to understand where It has come from and how to defeat It, drawing on a range of metaphysical influences, like the world-creating Turtle. It's final physical form is that of a giant spider, though even that is but an approximation of its "true" body. Between the Ritual of Chüd and the ultimate impossibility of representing It's physical form, the concrete horrors that have stalked the novel's first 1,000 pages become diffuse and defy easy categorization or comprehension as the novel draws to its close. In addition to the enormous size and scope of King's novel, these are among some of the most significant challenges—both narrative and structural—with which filmmakers adapting IT have had to contend.

Any adaptation of King's work can never be entirely separated from the larger context of King films, television series, miniseries, and other popular culture permutations over the years. Regardless of the screenwriters who reimagine or reframe the material and the directors who come to the text with an independent artistic vision, there will inevitably be the identification, for many viewers, of each work as a "Stephen King film," with this identification often foregrounded in marketing, with the author's name prefixed to the title or with advertising including phrases like "from the imagination of Stephen King."[2] This designation is a complicated and uneasy category. Adaptations of King have spanned a wide range of mediums, including film, television, comics, and, in the case of the Dark Tower-focused *Discordia*, an online game, making easy categorization or containment challenging. As Ian Nathan noted in his 2019 book *Stephen King at the Movies*: "No single author has been adapted more often than King. There are sixty-five existing movies, thirty television shows, and seven individual episodes (of multi-author anthology shows like *The Twilight Zone*) based on his work."[3] Further complicating this appellation, adaptations of King have varied widely in terms of quality, from the masterpiece of *The Shawshank Redemption* to the direct-to-video schlock of *Children of the Corn* and *Sometimes They Come Back* sequels.

Familiarity with King's work also offers readers a complex range of strategies for viewing, responding to, and "reading" these films. While some viewers and fans fail to move further than a fidelity-based "that's not how it was in the book" criticism, the source text and film taken together often provide new perspectives on familiar characters or a way of engaging with the film itself that leaves room for layers of meaning and interpretation. In Muschietti's *IT Chapter One*, for example, the missing child poster for Edward Corcoran is one poster of many, a child who is never seen on screen and whose sole role is in his poster effacing Betty Ripsom's (Katie Lunman), erasing her continued absence from larger discussions in Derry as the community moves on. However, in King's novel Corcoran was abused by his stepfather, who killed Eddie's younger brother Dorsey, a fact that underscores the human evil that exists right alongside It in Derry, both in the murder itself and in the town's inability—or refusal—to protect its children. This awareness does not fundamentally change the viewer's understanding of the film or its narrative, or present an obstacle for those viewers unfamiliar with King's novel. The Losers' discussion in *IT Chapter One* of part of Corcoran's body being found partially eaten implicates Pennywise or, at the very least, a combination of human abuse and It's feeding, but this narrative possibility does provide an opportunity to read these nuanced layers of meaning, place, and theme upon which Muschietti builds his films. From visual Easter eggs and self-referential lines to potential narrative asides such as that presented by Corcoran's missing poster in *IT*, any film based on King's work will almost inevitably build upon its source text in these complex and subtle ways, providing diverse viewer experiences and a range of potential engagements depending on the individual viewer's awareness, familiarity, and frames of reference.

Finally, it is worth considering King's own approach to and thoughts on adaptation. Over the course of his career, King has been generous in his assessment of adaptations of his work, with little expectation of point-by-point fidelity to his original text. For example, when viewers of the CBS series *Under the Dome* (2013–2015) objected that the show was veering too far afield from the narrative of King's novel, he wrote an open letter telling readers that "If you loved the book when you first read it, it's still there for your perusal. But that doesn't mean the TV series is bad, because it's not. In fact, it's very good."[4] King has liked some of the adaptations better than others and has been more directly involved in a handful of these, often indicated by a cameo, such as his appearance as the minister at Gage Creed's funeral in *Pet Sematary* (1989), the leader of an undead orchestra in Mick Garris's 1997 miniseries version of *The Shining*, and a pizza delivery guy in *Rose Red* (2002), with King also writing the screenplays for all three of these. In *IT Chapter Two*, King appears as a churlish shopkeeper, in a role that pokes gentle fun at King's celebrity author status and recognition. However, despite his personal thoughts or level of involvement in these adaptations, King's advice to disgruntled fans has consistently been "As for *you*, Constant Reader, feel free to take the original down from your bookshelf anytime you want. Nothing between the covers has changed a bit."[5]

Figure 1. King's cameo as a shopkeeper in IT Chapter Two

ADAPTATION, REMAKES, AND SEQUELS

As King's responses above note and as contemporary adaption theory argues, fidelity to a source text should not be the aim of adaptation, and any analysis of an adaptation based exclusively—or even predominantly—on the "criteria of fidelity"[6] will be a cursory comparison at best, lacking any substantive critical analysis. Instead, Linda Costanzo Cahir argues that adaptation should instead be seen as an act of dynamic "translation,"[7] an approach which highlights the fundamentally distinct features of literature and film, each with its own language, conventions, and form. An adaptation will never—and should not have the aim of being—the exact same story told in the exact same way, with the only difference being that it plays out on a screen rather than in the pages of a book. As Cahir notes: "Through the process of translation a fully new text—*a materially different entity*—is made, one that simultaneously has a strong relationship with its original source, yet is fully independent from it."[8] Filmmakers can take a range of approaches in this translation process. A literal translation aims to follow the letter of the original text as closely as possible; a traditional translation retains overall key traits while revising or negotiating others; and a radical translation provides a dynamic revision of the text at hand.[9] Each of these provide filmmakers with a wealth of strategies to consider and, in deciding what to keep and what to jettison, Cahir reminds readers that since everything cannot be represented, it is up to "each individual translator [who] must determine what is most crucial … The literal letter of the parent text? Its structure? Its unique music—its rhythms and sounds? Its meaning? Its accessibility to a popular audience? Its *beauty*?"[10] The elements a filmmaker chooses to prioritize guide all other choices of adaptation, and fidelity to a source text is just one of a diverse range of options (and arguably, the least interesting of the bunch).

In *Film Adaptation and Its Discontents*, Thomas Leitch provides a more extensive framework for considering adaptation. Drawing on Gérard Genette's theory of transtextuality, Leitch lays out a toolbox of approaches including celebration, adjustment, neoclassic imitation, revision, colonization, deconstruction, analogue, parody and pastiche, imitation, and allusion.[11] In analyzing adaptations of King's work in general and Muschietti's two films specifically, the two most productive of the approaches Leitch outlines are adjustment and revision. In adjusting a source text, a filmmaker has a range of strategies they can employ, including compressing an expansive narrative, expanding a short narrative, redressing particular elements, updating the text to a more modern time period, or superimposing a new framework onto a source text.[12] In considering Muschietti's *IT* films, compression is a necessary element of the adaptation process: even with the films' extensive run-times (135 minutes for *Chapter One* and 169 minutes for *Chapter Two*), translating a 1,000+ word novel inevitably requires careful selection and consolidation. Muschietti also updated the film's time period, shifting the 1950s childhood of King's original Losers to the mid-1980s, which both capitalizes on the current moment of 1980s popular cultural nostalgia and brings the Losers' return to Derry 27 years later into the contemporary moment. Time is central to the *IT* narrative and the release of *Chapter One* in 2017, exactly 27 years after Wallace's miniseries, also self-reflexively echoes this significance beyond the on-screen narrative in popular culture's return to and abiding fascination with Pennywise.

While adjustment provides a variety of approaches to working with the source text, revision foregrounds reassessment of the text itself.[13] As Leitch explains, revisions "differ from updates to the extent that they seek to rewrite the original, not simply to improve its ending or point out its contemporary relevance,"[14] in a move that again challenges the primacy of fidelity by adding new elements, drawing characters into sharper relief through additional backstories or perceptions, or reframing and reconceptualizing relationships that were undefined or unexplored in the source text.

One particularly significant use of revision and reassessment Muschietti employs in the *IT* films is the externalization of internal trauma. In King's novel, the Losers are often separated from one another, enduring It's onslaughts alone, with King's omniscient narration providing readers with insight into what the characters are thinking and feeling. However, while the film medium has a few resources for immersing the viewer in this subjective position, such as point of view shots and voiceover narration, for the most part these encounters and characters' internal processing of them must be externally communicated, with the experience of these horrors and the individual's response either inferred by the viewer through the actor's performance or narratively absorbed through conversations about that trauma, which has the doubled challenge of trying to articulate that which is often unspeakable. A particularly effective example of this externalization is in Bill's negotiation of his guilt over Georgie's death: from his speech to his friends as they prepare to enter the Neibolt Street house for the first time to his final conversation and confrontation with the monster masquerading as Georgie in the cistern in 1989 to the adult Bill facing his childhood self in *IT Chapter Two*, Bill's internal trauma is externalized, both vocally and performatively, articulating and reassessing this deeply personal guilt, sense of responsibility, and eventual healing.

Another salient example of revision in Muschietti's films is the reconsidered relationship between Richie and Eddie (or Reddie, as some fans have dubbed the duo). In *IT Chapter Two*, Muschietti reveals Richie's deep love for Eddie, creating a dynamic of same-sex desire that is represented but remains unspoken. This silencing is reinforced and brought into sharp relief by the brutal attack on Adrian Mellon (Xavier Dollan) that opens *IT Chapter Two*, who is singled out and beaten because he is gay, which acknowledges that, while significant progress has been made, the world is still not a safe place for many members of the LGBTQIA+ community. Through the dynamic process of revision, Muschietti is able to create and foreground new narratives and ways of seeing as he tells a familiar story, adding his own elements and layers of significance, characterization, narrative, and interpretation in his reassessment of King's text.

In addition to considering Muschietti's films as adaptations, it is also necessary to analyze them within the framework of the remake, with Wallace's 1990 miniseries as a touchstone and the initial adaptation of King's novel. The miniseries aired over two nights (Sunday, November 18 and Tuesday, November 20), with the first night's installment focused on the childhood experiences of the Losers Club and the second night's installment on their return to Derry as adults. Wallace's *IT* is inevitably shaped by the television medium, the first of "a decade of miniseries that tended to flatten King's imaginative flourishes to fit the advertiser-conscious prohibitions of television."[15] One of the most challenging elements of adapting *IT* for television were the Standards and Practices guidelines, particularly limitations on blood, gore, and representations of children in danger. As Simon Brown notes, this was a serious issue in adapting *IT*, as "Such endangerment is the premise of the 1950s narrative, and to avoid that would have effectively made King's novel unfilmable for TV."[16] ABC and Standards and Practices relaxed some of these restrictions for Wallace's miniseries, given the central narrative significance of children in danger, though how those representations were framed and packaged remained at the forefront of the adaptation process and are reflected in the miniseries' final product. The miniseries format also impacts the narrative structure of the film itself, with mini-climaxes and cliffhangers built in to accommodate commercial breaks and keep the audience from changing the channel, as well as a bigger cliffhanger between the first and second segment to ensure viewers would tune in for the second installment.

There is also Tim Curry's iconic performance as Pennywise in Wallace's miniseries to contend with in any remake or reimagining, as for a whole generation of viewers and horror fans, Curry became the singular face of the terrifying clown. Nathan argues that Curry's performance is the defining feature of Wallace's miniseries and that

"The reason this first edition of *IT* has endured is because Curry remains the most realized embodiment of psychopathic prankster Pennywise, and by extension the most complete of King's monsters."[17] With his stark white face, red nose, bushy circle of red hair, and vibrantly colored clown suit with orange pom-poms down the front, Curry's Pennywise is an iconic clown that very effectively combines the visual promise of fun with the underlying threat of danger and death. James Smythe reflects on this combination of merriment and terror, writing: "I love how innocuous he is, at first. How unsettling his performance is: when he's being jolly in luring Georgie to the sewer, there's something of the serial killer to him, rather than the immortal creature of the deadlights."[18] Curry's Pennywise embraces and embodies the carnivalesque, laughing maniacally and spinning a noisemaker, while always ensuring that the threat lurking beneath this performative surface remains constantly apparent and unforgettable. In this combination of allure and danger, "As played by Tim Curry, Pennywise, with his Brooklyn accent and leering delivery … suggests all kinds of potential horrors."[19] However, due to Standards and Practices restrictions, in Wallace's miniseries, "The violence that is explicit in King's novel becomes implicit,"[20] leaving the vast majority of these horrors to the viewer's imagination.

Given the cult classic status of Wallace's miniseries—and, more specifically, Curry's performance as Pennywise—any consideration of Muschietti's films must also consider the critical position of *IT Chapter One* and *Chapter Two* as remakes. As Constantine Verevis explains, "the concept of *remaking* is never simply a quality of texts, but is the secondary result of broader discursive activity."[21] Like adaptation, remaking is a dynamically engaged process of selecting, condensing, revising, and amplifying specific elements of a preceding text. In his consideration of remakes, Verevis outlines three categories through which remakes can be productively addressed: the industrial, the textual, and the critical.[22] Industrially speaking, Muschietti's *IT* films fall into the category of "*the acknowledged, transformed remake*,"[23] in the awareness of audiences' preexisting familiarity with Wallace's miniseries and Muschietti's commitment to updating and revising the narrative. However, while this familiarity is recognized, it does not serve as a goal or bar for replication, as Muschietti's films occupy the textual position of what Verevis calls a "*Readaptation* … [in which] the remake ignores or treats as inconsequential earlier cinematic adaptations,"[24] though they remain engaged with that earlier work as a result of audience familiarity and expectations, prompting Leitch to identify a triangulation that includes audience recognition of the source text and the earlier film(s), upon which Verevis builds.[25] In this readaptation approach, for example, Muschietti is aware that viewers are likely to have the image of Curry as Pennywise established in their minds and rather than trying to replicate that image in a new film with a new actor, with *IT Chapter One* and *Two*, Muschietti and Skarsgård present a reimagined Pennywise, with "a very different sort of clown: less terrible old-timey Brooklyn accent, more unnervingly juddery Victoriana ghoul."[26] With this muted palette, a painted smile and distended lower lip often dripping with drool, and unnervingly off-center eyes that change from blue to yellow as It moves to attack, Skarsgård's Pennywise readapts the terrifying clown, rather than making any attempt to update or emulate Curry's iconic look.

There is the also notion of the remake as a critical category, which foregrounds the intertextual engagement of the remake with the preceding text. Through this approach, remakes critically engage the reader through "the explicit and recognisable intertextual quotation of plot motifs and stylistic features peculiar to earlier film versions."[27] This is true even when the remake chooses to go in a dramatically different direction through readaptation, such as Muschietti's synthesized narrative structure and the creation of new elements of characterization and relationships that reframe the source text and earlier adaptations. There are several examples of intertextual engagement between Muschietti's films and Wallace's miniseries that foreground a reading of Muschietti's films as remakes within Verevis's critical framework, with Muschietti's film echoing elements from Wallace's miniseries such as adult Mike's (Tim Reid) voiceover establishing the shift between the world of children and that of adults; visually doubled elements that transition between the adult Losers and their flashbacks in the first installment of the miniseries, such as Bill's (Richard Thomas and Jonathan Brandis) hand pressed to the side of his face and Stan (Richard Masur and Ben Heller) nervously tugging his ear; and the importance of the Losers positioned in a circle as they comfort Bill in the Barrens, resist Pennywise in the sewers as children, and stand against Pennywise's onslaught in the library as adults.

Finally, there is the critical analysis of sequels. While the traditional definition of a sequel addresses films that "recycle the characters of a previously successful story in order to exploit them, by telling what happened to them after the end of their first adventure,"[28] Verevis argues that these films deserve much more critical attention, one that foregrounds "the film sequel as a complex situation: a function of a *network* of commercial interests, textual strategies, critical vocabularies, and historical contexts."[29] Sequels are an established tradition of the horror film genre, with *Halloween*, *Friday the 13th*, *Nightmare on Elm Street*, *Scream*, and the *Conjuring* franchises, among others. However, while Muschietti's *IT Chapter Two* does provide a continuation of the Losers Club's story, in many ways *Chapter Two* is not a sequel at all, but rather a continuation of the narrative that enfolds and synthesizes the earlier film, with Muschietti noting of *IT Chapter One* that "In my mind this was always like the first half of a story"[30] and King referring to *IT Chapter Two* as "the second half of one unified story."[31]

IT Chapter Two reframes and reconsiders the action of *Chapter One* in ways that make the first film impossible to fully understand or engage with without the additional interconnected narrative provided in the second film. While countless horror films end with the danger amorphously unresolved—the monster escaped, the madman having disappeared into the night—with Bill's imprecation to his friends to "Swear if It isn't dead, if It ever comes back, we'll come back too" at the conclusion of *IT Chapter One*, the story is overtly established as unfinished, open-ended. Rather than leaving the conclusion open for the *possibility* of a sequel, *Chapter One* ends with an *imperative* for the story's continuation, an explicit acknowledgement that this is *not* the end, underscored by the addition of "Chapter One" to the film's title that appears prior to the closing credits. This interconnection of the narratives of these two films is clearly indicated in their titling as well, with *Chapter One* and *Chapter Two* denoting two parts of the same interconnected and continuing narrative. This approach is further developed by the synthesis of the Losers' childhood memories and adult recollections in *IT Chapter Two*, as forgotten or repressed memories from their separate experiences during that terrifying childhood summer are filled in, developing the story of *IT Chapter One* in structurally and narratively essential ways, synthesizing the two films into a single, extended work, with each relying on the other for completion and comprehension. As a result, while their separate narratives and structures will be central to the analysis that follows, rather than identifying and engaging with *IT Chapter Two* as a traditional sequel, I will address and critically analyze *IT Chapter One* and *Chapter Two* as a singular cohesive narrative.

Notes

1. Quoted in Bev Vincent, *The Stephen King Illustrated Companion: Manuscripts, Correspondence, Drawings, and Memorabilia from the Master of Modern Horror* (New York: Metro Books, 2009), 84.
2. Ian Nathan, *Stephen King at the Movies: A Complete History of the Film and Television Adaptations from the Master of Horror* (London: Palazzo, 2019), 8.
3. Nathan, 7.
4. Stephen King, "A Letter from Stephen," *StephenKing.com*, 2013, https://www.stephenking.com/promo/utd_on_ tv/letter.html.
5. King, "A Letter from Stephen," original emphasis.
6. Thomas Leitch, *Film Adaptation and Its Discontents: From* Gone with the Wind *to* The Passion of the Christ (Baltimore: Johns Hopkins University Press, 2007), 139.
7. Linda Costanzo Cahir, *Literature into Film: Theory and Practical Approaches* (Jefferson, NC: McFarland & Company, 2006), 13.
8. Cahir, 14, original emphasis.
9. Cahir, 16–17.
10. Cahir, 15, original emphasis.
11. Leitch, 96–123.
12. Leitch, 98–100.
13. Leitch, 106.
14. Leitch, 106.
15. Nathan, 73.
16. Simon Brown, *Screening Stephen King: Adaptation and the Horror Genre in Film and Television* (Austin: University of Texas Press, 2018), 158.
17. Nathan, 75.
18. James Smythe, "Fears of a Clown: Why the Original It Will Always Be the Best," *The Guardian*, 4 Sept. 2019, https://www.theguardian.com/tv-and-radio/2019/sep/04/it-clown-miniseries-tim-curry-stephen-king.
19. Brown, 158.
20. Brown, 158.
21. Constantine Verevis, *Film Remakes* (Edinburgh: Edinburgh University Press, 2005), 45, original emphasis.

22. Verevis, *Film Remakes*, 2. It is also important to note the significant differences in the filmmaking and industry approaches between Wallace's miniseries and Muschietti's films: there are different expectations for television vs. feature films, particularly in terms of budget, cast, and audience. There is also a significant difference in the time frame of each work's release, with two years passing between *IT Chapter One* and *Chapter Two*, as opposed to the two days that separated the airing of the miniseries installments, with audience responses to *IT Chapter One* inevitably influencing the making of the second film and resulting in a new set of expectations and anticipations for *IT Chapter Two*.

23. Verevis, *Film Remakes*, 9, original emphasis.

24. Verevis, *Film Remakes*, 12, original emphasis.

25. Verevis, *Film Remakes*, 12–13.

26. Smythe.

27. Verevis, *Film Remakes*, 24.

28. Umberto Eco, "Innovation and Repetition: Between Modern and Post-Modern Aesthetics," *Daedalus*, vol. 114, no. 4 (1985), 167.

29. Constantine Verevis, "Redefining the Sequel: The Case of the (Living) Dead," *Second Takes: Critical Approaches to the Film Sequel*, edited by Carolyn Jess-Cooke and Constantine Verevis (Albany: State University of New York Press, 2010), 12, original emphasis.

30. "The Summers of IT—Chapter Two: IT Ends," *IT Chapter Two*, directed by Constantine Nasr (Rivendell Films, 2020).

31. Quoted in Karishma Shetty, "EXCLUSIVE: Stephen King on IT: Chapter 2: It's Not a Sequel; It's the Second Half of One Unified Story," *Pinkvilla*, 6 Sept. 2019, https://www.pinkvilla.com/entertainment/exclusives/exclusive-stephen-king-it-chapter-2-it-s-not-sequel-it-s-second-half-one-unified-story-471962.

Chapter 2: Coming Home to Horror

The foundational horror of It is its corruption of Derry itself: It's influence is all-encompassing, pre-dating the founding of the town, underlying its very existence and fundamentally shaping the character of both Derry and the people who live there. It's power and predation are in direct opposition to Derry as It feeds on their children but, at the same time, It is also a fundamental part of Derry's identity and the community itself.

Derry looms large in Muschietti's films. Sweeping overhead shots take in the town as a whole, amplifying the imagery of small-town nostalgia, with the reassuring familiarity of its tree-lined streets and red-brick downtown. *IT Chapter One* opens on an overhead shot of Bill Denbrough's residential neighborhood, with its spacious and well-tended single-family homes and beautiful front lawns, before cutting to Bill's bedroom and the brothers' construction of Georgie's paper boat, inviting viewers into the seemingly predictable and comforting domestic space. The opening scenes of *IT Chapter Two* feature establishing shots of Derry's downtown, the library, and the town square with its Paul Bunyan statue.

Figure 2. Downtown Derry

In addition to these contextualizing, big-picture shots of Derry as a whole that open *Chapter Two*, Muschietti also features a range of street-level establishing shots, positioning the viewer on the same ground the Losers themselves walk as the camera navigates a darkened school hallway, the river, the alley, and a brick wall lined with missing children posters. In lingering on these images of Derry to provide the viewer with an intimate sense of place, Muschietti is visually building on King's descriptive approach to detailing his uncanny towns like Derry, Castle Rock, and Jerusalem's Lot, through which, James Arthur Anderson notes, "the reader knows more about [these towns] than he could know about his own hometown even,"[1] which creates a sense of Derry as "hyperreal."[2] The viewer is immersed in Derry, engaged with these familiar places and capable of navigating this fictional geography, all within the larger context of the uncanny that results from the combination of nostalgic familiarity and ever-present supernatural danger.[3]

Finally, Derry is brought into its sharpest focus through the Losers' collective engagement with it, as they venture into, explore, and uncover the secrets of Derry's hidden corners. In some ways, this exploration is empowering and proprietary, an act of claiming a space for themselves on the margins of a town that cares little for their safety or well-being, as they walk single-file through the Barrens, swim in the quarry, and hang out in the clubhouse Ben builds for them. Each of these spaces and the Losers' connections within them establish an order and connection that the Losers almost immediately fall back into when they are reunited as adults, reconnecting with their friends, their childhood selves, and their relationship with Derry, despite the changes in the places themselves, like the warning sign-posted barrier that now prevents jumpers at the quarry and the door to the clubhouse that collapses under Ben's (Jay Ryan) feet.

While the Barrens, the quarry, and the clubhouse are sites of safety and togetherness for the Losers, Muschietti also provides intimate and detailed shots of other, more terrifying places, including the house on Neibolt Street, the sewer tunnels, and the cistern. As places the Losers are not meant to go—and which are hidden, for the most part, from the citizens of Derry in general—venturing into these places is an act of defiance, a journey into the unknown that makes attention to detail even more crucial to the Losers' survival, a necessity that invests viewers once more in Anderson's "hyperreal"[4] perspective, though on a smaller, more intimate scale. Another key distinction is that while the other places around Derry that feature prominently in this established sense of place are public (i.e. the library, the school, the pharmacy), when the Losers enter the house on Neibolt Street and venture into the sewers below, they are separated from that larger world, entering a liminal space that simultaneously is Derry and is *not* Derry, is *beyond* Derry. They are unfixed, unmoored. There is no possibility of anyone seeing or finding them; there is no hope of rescue if things go badly, which means they have no one to rely upon but themselves and one another. The Losers are not even safe within their own homes, with these private, domestic spaces becoming places of danger, as Eddie's mother (Molly Atkinson) confines him, Bev's father (Stephen Bogaert) abuses her, and Bill must wrestle with his isolation, grief, and guilt following Georgie's death.

The notion of place is even more complicated as Pennywise's presence and influence have a significant impact on this sense of place and the ways in which the Losers— and the other children of Derry—occupy these spaces. When It appears, the lines between public vs. private, visible vs. invisible, and safety vs. danger become blurred and unreliable, with isolated pockets of Derry becoming liminal spaces of their own, as the Losers are isolated and under threat, even within ostensibly safe public places, as the reality of Pennywise's predation is hidden from view and Derry's citizens see nothing, remain unaware, or look the other way. Georgie *should* be safe on a public, residential street, but the woman who comes out onto her porch in the rain sees him crouching in front of the sewer opening and turns away. Ben *should* be safe in the library, but as Pennywise chases him through the basement stacks, Ben is drawn into a tangled maze, separated from the everyday realities just upstairs. Victoria Fuller (Ryan Kiera Armstrong) *should* be safe at the baseball game, within earshot of a stand's worth of cheering spectators, but once she is drawn into the shadows beneath the bleachers, it is almost as if that larger world ceases to exist. In each of these cases, the child in question is first separated from the "real" world of Derry, isolated and alone, then drawn into the liminal space that Pennywise occupies as they follow either their desire or their curiosity: Georgie's boat, the balloon and eggs Ben sees in the library, the firefly Victoria chases.

This liminality is echoed by the dream logic of some of the adult Losers' recollections of their childhood horrors as well, such as the nightmares Eddie discovers in the basement of Keene's Pharmacy and Ben's encounter with It in the summer-empty school.

Pennywise's presence influences and complicates any understanding of Derry as a fixed and knowable place: it is familiar yet defined by its dark secrets, physical yet completely fluid and changeable. As Muschietti provides viewers with a range of perspectives on Derry—from sweeping establishing shots to street-level views and the more intimate, embodied perspectives of places both public and private—that fundamental mystery remains. Early in *IT Chapter Two*, for example, Muschietti's camera zooms in on the black mouth of the storm drain where Georgie was murdered, immersing viewers in this darkness only to transition to the bright lights and frenetic sounds of Derry's Canal Days Festival. Everything is interconnected, though the connections are often not what the viewer might expect, and nowhere is safe.

Building on Muschietti's visual representation of Derry and his approach to establishing this sense of place, the interconnection of It and Derry operate on multiple levels, through the identification of Derry as a traditionally Gothic "Bad Place," the interconnection of past and present, and It's influence on the people of Derry.

THE GOTHIC "BAD PLACE"

Setting is a key component in the Gothic tradition, transcending physical or geographical place to operate both symbolically and thematically as well. In *Danse Macabre*, his non-fiction consideration of the horror genre, King provides his own take on what he calls "the Bad Place,"[5] arguing that it often acts as a kind of "psychic battery,"[6] holding onto the memories, emotions, and violence that have occurred there. Though King explores this idea specifically with regard to haunted houses in *Danse Macabre*, the same could be said of many of King's uncanny small Maine towns, including Derry and Castle Rock.

Derry is an undeniably Bad Place. As Ben tells his friends in *IT Chapter One*, "Derry's not like any town I've ever been in before." Derry's past has been punctuated by mysterious disappearances, horrific acts of violence, and a litany of missing and murdered children. The 27-year cycle of violence illustrates that this is not an isolated occurrence: it has happened before and it will happen again. Though Dustin Thomason is talking about Castle Rock when he asks "who stays in a town like that?",[7] the same question could be asked of Derry. Derry residents' memories are long and they are well aware of this history, but that knowledge changes nothing. They ignore it, silence it, and try to forget it, and for the most part, they do not leave and they do not fight.

While the Gothic place can be overtly horrific, it can just as easily hide beneath a pleasant façade, with "places of destruction instead of order, or of order masking ruin."[8] Derry arguably does both, with its idyllic town square and tree-lined streets in sharp contrast to the horrors of the house on Neibolt Street, for example. Derry is clearly a place of disorder and disruption, evidenced by the missing children and gruesome discoveries, like the mutilated body of Adrian Mellon, though these dangers are masked behind the familiarity of the nostalgically imagined small town, particularly in *IT Chapter One*. As A.O. Scott points out: "Derry, with its redbrick storefronts and its quirks and kinks, seems like a genuinely nice place to live in spite of the fact that its citizens, children in particular, turn up missing or maimed at an alarming rate."[9] In the wake of these horrors, Derry puts on the proper community face, signaling their collective concern with the litany of missing children posters that adorn walls and telephone poles, but the darker reality is that these are soon papered over with those of other children who have more recently gone missing, with Bill noting of Betty Ripsom's now-covered poster that "It's like she's been forgotten" (*IT Chapter One*). As a volunteer puts up a missing poster for Patrick Hockstetter in *IT Chapter One*, her face is placid and resigned, a woman going through the motions rather than driven by authentic sorrow, worry, or hope of his return. One exception to this pattern of passivity is Betty Ripsom's mother, who waits for her missing daughter outside the school, watchful and grief-stricken, though she is clearly noted as an anomaly. Even Bill's own parents have resigned themselves to Georgie's death, with Bill's father (Geoffrey Pounsett) becoming angry and dismissive at Bill holding on to the slim hope that Georgie could still be alive or, if he is dead, that his body could be recoverable, which would offer the possibility for closure the Denbrough family has been denied. In the wake of horror, the town and its citizens move on, as they must, but the sheer volume of Derry's losses and the seeming ease of their forgetting indicate indifference and ambivalence, rather than heroic perseverance.

In addition to these mysterious losses and the supernatural threat of It, there is plenty of human evil in Derry as well, including racism and violent homophobia.[10] While Bowers and his gang abuse each member of the Losers Club—and many of the other children of Derry besides—Bowers' attacks on Mike are clearly racially motivated. In *IT Chapter One* Bowers and his friends attempt to run Mike down with a car, after which Bowers screams at Mike to "Stay the fuck outta my town" and throws a lit cigarette at him, with his proprietary definition of Derry one of whiteness, violence, and exclusion. The danger of this real-world and racially motivated violence is further complicated by the supernatural influence of Pennywise, who had been preparing to attack Mike, an encounter that left Mike frozen in the alley outside the butcher shop and perfectly positioned for Bowers' and his gang's attack, in a combination of supernatural and human horror. Beyond this overt violence and abuse, the citizens of Derry also marginalize and denigrate Mike, particularly in their telling of the story of his parents' deaths, dismissing them as mentally ill drug addicts who died in an apartment fire they set while high. This dominant narrative erases the tragedy, posthumously villainizing and ostracizing Mike's parents and, by extension, Mike as well, who is left with an understanding of himself and his family that is deeply flawed, informed by silence and shame. Mike sees himself through Derry's eyes and views his own past through the lens of this racist narrative construction, which makes it impossible for him to see or understand the truth of who his parents were and their tragic loss well into his adulthood, a flawed understanding that impacts his relationship with his grandfather (Steven Williams) and his own identity.

The attack on Adrian Mellon that opens *IT Chapter Two* is another example of the human hate and violence that characterize Derry. Adrian and his boyfriend Don Hagarty (Taylor Frey) are pursued and harassed by a group of homophobic young men, who then attack Adrian. The attack itself is unrelentingly brutal as they punch and kick Adrian, knock away his inhaler when he has an asthma attack and is struggling to breathe, and then throw him over the bridge and into the swiftly flowing river below. This is one of the most controversial scenes of Muschietti's two *IT* films. With LGBTQIA+ characters frequently featuring as either sensationalized victims or villains in horror films, this concern is well-founded. Queerness in the horror genre has often been positioned "in the role of the Other,"[11] defined as different and therefore, dangerous. As Iman Jaroudi argues, "What is sinister about horror is its capacity to throw queer characters in as purely victims or purely villains, without providing the same development and context to them as to cishet characters."[12] Within this framework, LGBTQIA+ characters are shown as being either expendable or monstrous, denied the fully developed characterization, narrative trajectory, and value of their straight counterparts, with their deaths too often exploitative or sensationally represented.

The young men's cruelty and sadism as they attack Adrian is horrific and Muschietti's representation of this violence is unflinching. However, rather than presenting this act of violence in a sensationalized or gratuitous way, Muschietti keeps Adrian and Don's humanity at the forefront, communicating both the physical and emotional anguish of this violent assault, while making it undeniably clear that some of Derry's human residents are just as horrifying—if not more so—than Pennywise himself. This scene is drawn from King's novel, which was in turn directly inspired by the 1984 murder of Charlie Howard, a young gay man who was attacked in much the same way, violently beaten and then thrown off of a bridge to his death in the water below in Bangor, Maine (the real-world inspiration for King's Derry).[13] While horror often takes viewers out of the everyday, in this case art directly imitates life, with King using fiction and Muschietti using film to tell the story of real-life violence, the tragic death of Charlie Howard, and the threats LGBTQIA+ individuals often face. When asked about this scene, Muschietti noted:

> It's a very, very devastating event. Not only because of the outcome, but also it has the implications of the social undertone. It's a hate crime ... which is something that resonates in the times that we're living in and at the time that we lived before. It's a sequence that will have impact on a couple of different levels, I think.[14]

Both within the narrative of the film and the context of its contemporary world, this scene is significant in recognizing the multiple levels of evil at play in Derry with It's return, as well as forcing viewers to face the reality of real-world anti-LGBTQIA+ violence head on, instead of offering the opportunity to follow in the Derry citizens' footsteps and look the other way, ignore it, or refuse to see it, whether on screen or in real life.

While it is presented as a horrifying tragedy in its own right, Adrian Mellon's murder also provides a larger framework for understanding Richie's silence. One of the big revelations in *IT Chapter Two*—and one of Muschietti's own additions to King's established narrative—is that Richie is gay. In one of the flashback scenes of *IT Chapter Two*, Bowers berates Richie, threatening him and calling him a "faggot" when he finds Richie playing video games with his cousin in the local arcade. Richie conceals both this traumatic encounter and his sexual identity from his friends, a choice that is almost unquestioningly driven by small-town homophobia, the discourse surrounding gay men and AIDS in the 1980s,[15] and hate crimes like the murder of Charlie Howard in 1984. However, as an adult, Richie still maintains this silence, despite his escape from Derry, his love for Eddie, and a more inclusive and accepting twenty-first-century culture. While this continued secrecy might initially seem inexplicable and unnecessary to a contemporary audience, the brutal attack on Adrian Mellon reminds viewers that such hate crimes are not relegated to the past, a reality that was especially pronounced during Donald Trump's presidency, in which the United States experienced a "43% increase in anti-LGBTQ hate groups in 2019."[16] Richie's own recollection of and reflection on his childhood experiences highlight his internalized shame and terror, an indicator of the ways in which his life and experiences in Derry have indelibly marked him, an intimate personal reflection within the larger scope of systemic anti-LGBTQIA+ rejection, abuse, and violence.

PAST AND PRESENT

Derry epitomizes the Gothic "Bad Place," with acts of repression, abuse, and violence happening both in the shadows and in the open. Derry's character is fixed and immutable: bad things have happened, are happening, and will continue to happen in a never-ending cycle. The horrors of the Gothic place are impossible to separate from those of the past and, as a result, are inescapable. These dark truths are an integral part of the place's identity and any action that occurs there does so under the burden of that dark history, it secrets, and the myriad implications of both. Muschietti builds on "King's dark and elaborate history of Derry, Maine [which] chronicles many of the most brutal and inhumane events which have occurred during the past three centuries."[17] Derry's past abounds with cyclical violence, as every 27 years a new horror occurs, including the murder of the Bradley Gang, the Derry Iron Works explosion, the burning of the Black Spot, the Losers' childhood horrors, and their return to Derry as adults. Textual artifacts of this history feature predominantly throughout both films, including closeup shots of the book *A History of Old Derry*, historical documents, and newspaper articles both past and present, making the town's history and the Losers' overt exploration of it central to the narrative in gaining an understanding of Derry and It.

In *IT Chapter One*, Ben's research takes him back to the historical genesis of Derry, with the founding of the township. As Ben tells his fellow Losers of Derry's original settlers, "they all disappeared without a trace" (*IT Chapter One*). The walls of Ben's room visually echo the investigative process, with myriad connections, overlappings, and unanswered questions, making it possible for the Losers to physically navigate the historical narrative, shifting from one element to another, reflecting on text, image, and legend as they work to understand the town in which they live and the evil that has shaped it throughout the entirety of its history. Ben's fascination with Derry's history and Mike's continuation of this research as an adult in *IT Chapter Two* highlight the larger tradition of which the Losers are one small part, while also foregrounding the ways in which past and present are synthesized.

Figure 3. Navigating Derry's history

In *IT Chapter Two*, Bev meets the monster in the guise of an old woman in her childhood apartment, who constructs an alternate history of Pennywise as her father and a traveling circus clown named Bob Gray. As Mrs Kersh (Joan Gregson) reminds Bev, in Derry, "No one who dies here ever really dies" (*IT Chapter Two*). While there is clear subterfuge and narrative construction at work in Bev's conversation with the old woman, this pronouncement is undeniably true: It is a returning, cyclical evil, but even the more prosaic dead are animated into their own horrific returns, like Georgie Denbrough and Patrick Hockstetter. This synthesis of past and present is echoed in the structure of *IT Chapter Two*, as well as in the interconnection of the two films, with *Chapter Two* acting as a continuation of a single, cohesive narrative rather than as a traditional sequel. As the adult Losers discover when they return to Derry, they have not really left their childhood selves behind (even if they have been temporarily forgotten) and the past will invariably intrude upon and influence the present, as shown through their own reminiscences and the flashbacks that add missing pieces to the narrative presented by *IT Chapter One* and provide a new lens for both the Losers and the viewers to consider that previously established version of events.

One of the foundational artifacts of Ben's research is the map of Derry township, which provides insight and important information missing from the Losers' earlier sleuthing: the location of the well house. This map is another illustrative example of the synthesis of past and present, as the Losers are able to combine it with the contemporary map of the sewers that Bill has filched from his father's office. In both boys' fascination with these maps and their attempts to claim the knowledge the maps promise—with Ben seeking to understand Derry's dark colonial history and Bill working to figure out where his brother's body might have ended up—they are both connecting with and distancing themselves from the horrors of Derry's past and present, turning the dangers around them into a concrete and objective text they can consider, manipulate, and control. These two maps provide the Losers with one of their first collective breakthroughs, with Ben's map slide-projected onto the map of the sewer tunnels enabling them to solve the mystery of the well house and pointing them toward It's lair in the house on Neibolt Street. While this sense of control is limited—as the Losers discover when Pennywise takes over the slide projector, corrupts Bill's family photos, and explodes from the makeshift screen to terrorize them—the knowledge they have gained and the power this affords them are essential as they take their next steps toward finding and fighting Pennywise. The synthesis of these two maps is a particularly effective illustration of the ways in which the past and the present can never be fully separated from one another in Derry: they must know and understand both in order to move forward, just as when they come back as adults, they must return to their childhood memories and selves in order to be successful.

Ben's adolescent research traced Derry back to its foundation, a colonial and predominantly white definition of "civilization," with only a passing note of "rumors of Indians but no sign of an attack" in his consideration of the settlers' disappearance. Mike's research in *IT Chapter Two* is more expansive, with his inclusion of the Shokopiwah tribe's experiences echoing his own self-identification as "an outsider" (*IT Chapter One*).[18] When Mike tells Bill about his conversations with the Shokopiwah in *IT Chapter Two*, Mike frames himself as a humble seeker of knowledge, telling Bill that "They helped me on my journey." However, despite being able to identify and empathize with the Shokopiwah's position outside of the dominant culture, Mike's treatment of the Shokopiwah people is problematic and exploitative. He gains the information he has sought, being taken into their traditions and shown a vision of It's arrival that effectively reframes Derry's history, but Mike's understanding is not his own as he instead co-opts the Shokopiwah experience, his body language directly echoing that of the Shokopiwah person standing behind him, both with their right arms outstretched as they survey It's landing.

The most exploitative part of Mike's interaction with the Shokopiwah, however, is his theft of the early eighteenth-century Shokopiwah ritual vase that pictorially recounts the Ritual of Chüd. Mike appropriates not just the Shokopiwah people's knowledge, but this sacred physical artifact of the tribe as well. Once he has established possession, Mike then does the unthinkable and destroys the final side of the vase, the one that depicts the failure of the ritual, erasing the Shokopiwah's confrontation with It not only from the story he shares with his fellow Losers but from their own cultural artifact as well, rewriting the history and narrative that are central to his plan moving forward. While Mike's actions and exploitation of the Shokopiwah are those of an individual, his sense of entitlement and this abuse echo Derry's own treatment of the Shokopiwah people, who exist at the town's margins. Even Mike's theft is echoed in Derry's larger appropriation of the Shokopiwah's Native American culture, with the artifacts on display in the library, including a tomahawk that is overtly foregrounded with a close-up shot that prioritizes Bill's gaze and that later conveniently becomes useful when Mike is attacked by Henry Bowers. The Shokopiwah and their culture are appropriated, displayed, and put to unintended use by members of the dominant culture and Derry at large.

The sins of the past and the violence of the present can never be effectively separated from one another in Derry specifically or within the larger Gothic tradition. It's presence reasserts itself every 27 years, but the horrors of each cycle blur together and overlap, such as Ben being pursued by the headless boy from the long-ago Derry Iron Works explosion and the adult Losers once more encountering Betty Ripsom's animated, dismembered body when they return to Derry. The adult Losers are also haunted by their own childhood terrors, which seem to exist in dual worlds. For example, in *IT Chapter Two* Henry Bowers is both the nightmare bully of their childhoods and also the escaped mental patient who tries to kill them, while Bill's horror doubles as he encounters both young Georgie and the boy Dean (Luke Roessler) who, like Georgie, Bill is unable to save. Every element of Derry's past, including its previous inhabitants and every instance of violence or cruelty, remains. Derry has a dark history and none of it rests easy, returning and repeating in tandem with It's cycle of violence, never truly laid to rest.

As the Losers rediscover their childhood experiences, the familiar streets, and their forgotten terrors when they return to Derry as adults, they experience this bridging of past and present as well. Much of this occurs through their remembering—both individually and collectively—but even when their final confrontation with It is over, the lasting impression of Derry endures. As Bill, Bev, Richie, Ben, and Mike walk through downtown Derry one last time, they stop to look at their reflections in a plate glass window emblazoned with the tourism slogan "Derry is calling you" to see their childhood selves, joined once more by Eddie and Stan, gazing back at them, a reminder of who they are, the connections that unite them, and the place they have called home.

Figure 4. Synthesizing past and present in the Losers' reflection

THE PEOPLE OF DERRY

In terms of the Gothic place, in addition to serving as a setting and the site of intersections of past and present horrors, place also becomes entangled with and influences the people who live there, with John Sears noting that in King's work specifically, "places both identify with and become identified with character and with groups of characters."[19] As Sears explains:

> King's Gothic adapts and extends a deliberate confusion of internal, character-psychological or group-dynamic features with external, spatial/topological features. Such confusion is structural to the Gothic genre's extension and complication of notions of sympathetic background. Place constitutes [...] both a complex form or expression of otherness and a territory in which otherness may reside. It both contains and fails to contain otherness.[20]

Everyone in Derry is marked by that sense of belonging and the unique nature of Derry. The Losers' t-shirts sport the logos of local businesses like the Tracker Brothers Trucking Company, Freese's Department Store, and the Bike & Cycle Shoppe (*IT Chapter One*) and the local baseball team has a large and enthusiastic crowd of fans in their stands (*IT Chapter Two*). There is a local children's show, the *Derry Children's Hour*, which appears regularly on televisions throughout both films, establishing a shared local discourse, which It co-opts and influences. Notably, no children are shown watching this program through either of Muschietti's films—with the exception of Henry's brief attention to it as he prepares to murder his father—though it appears on the television sets of several adult characters, including Eddie's mother, Henry's father (Stuart Hughes), and Bev's father.[21] These details are part of the everyday existence of Derry citizens: the familiar images and rhythms of their lives, part of what makes Derry uniquely Derry.

Figure 5: Mr Keene's Pennywise-ish leer

However, beyond It's destructive influence—whether as Pennywise or in one of its countless other guises—the people of Derry are capable of great violence and evil as well, as demonstrated by the murder of Adrian Mellon and the abuse Bev suffers at the hands of her father, among others. It is unclear to what degree (if any) the violence of the people of Derry can be truly separated from It's influence, blurring the lines between human and supernatural evils. One level of this engagement is in "the way certain Derry townsfolk resemble Skargård's Pennywise, playing into the notion as expressed in the original book that It is everywhere."[22] As Brian W. Smith notes, Eddie's mother, the pharmacist Mr Keene (Joe Bostick), and an old woman in the library "all seemingly share impish facial similarities and the staring eyes of Pennywise"[23] in isolated moments of conflict with the children they encounter. Mrs Kasprak's gaze shifts ominously when she tries to prevent Eddie from leaving the house and rejoining his friends, Mr Keene looks at Bev with a sexualizing and acquisitive leer, and the old woman watches Ben with a predatory glee as he reads about Derry's dark history.[24] These are subtle and telling moments, interactions that let the viewer know that "something's terribly wrong with Derry's adult population,"[25] who seem to be particularly susceptible to It's power, temporarily embodying the evil that defines Derry, expanding the monster's scope, and further underscoring the interconnection between Derry and the people who live there.

It also exerts its influence over the people of Derry through complacency. Even citizens who would likely never hurt a child themselves are lulled into looking the other way, like the couple in *IT Chapter One* that drive past Henry Bowers' gang attacking Ben as they turn away, ignore what they have seen, and drive on, with It's direct influence indicated by the red balloon that rises to fill the car's back window. While this is a single, isolated incident, Derry is defined by this type of complacency, in its lack of a response to the sheer number of missing and murdered children. As young Bill asks his friends as he prepares to enter the house on Neibolt Street in *IT Chapter One*, when another child inevitably goes missing, "Are you just gonna pretend it isn't happening, like everyone else in this town?" Ignoring these horrors are a Derry tradition, one in which the vast majority of adults seem well-versed. Much of Derry's violence happens right out in the open: Georgie Denbrough and Adrian Mellon are killed on public streets, unnoticed and unsaved, while the boy Dean is killed in the depths of the funhouse's mirror maze, right in the heart of the civic pride of Derry's Canal Days Festival. While the people of Derry effectively go through the motions by instating a curfew and posting missing children posters, for example, there is no heightened vigilance, no outrage or demand for action or justice. Violence abounds, children are murdered, and life goes on.

However, it is undeniable that plenty of horror would exist in Derry even without It's influence or the town's identification as a Gothic Bad Place. No supernatural catalyst is needed for bullies to torment their peers. Parents physically, sexually, and emotionally abuse their children without It's influence. Mr Keene sexually objectifies Bev. Gretta actively enjoys tormenting Bev and Eddie. Anti-LGBTQIA+ violence is all too real. Even in It's control of Henry Bowers, there are a range of real-world influences that contribute to Henry's breaking point, including his father's humiliation and abuse.[26]

It may wield its influence to cause the people of Derry to do bad things or, conversely, It may be attracted to and feed upon the violence they are already committing and would commit with or without its influence. As Tony Magistrale notes of this integral connection as developed in King's novel: "Anytime an act of violence or cruelty occurs in Derry, Pennywise is present to celebrate it, to participate in it, and to reap the power accrued from the act itself."[27] One instance in which this interconnection is uncertain is in the murder of Adrian Mellon, who is brutally beaten and thrown off of a bridge, where Pennywise waits on the shore to claim him. Adrian's attackers' voices overlap as they beat him, an auditory cacophony that contributes to the chaos of the scene. Within this jumble of voices, the young boy Chris Unwin's (Katie Lunman)[28] voice is particularly frenetic, with its heightened pitch and near-hysteria almost mimicking Pennywise's own giggling cadence as Chris cheers his older friends on. Adrian's attackers are depicted as clearly monstrous, though this also raises the possibility of It's subtle influence, with Pennywise waiting below to feed. However, with the fundamental uncertainty and lack of narrative resolution on this point, it is arguably just as likely that Pennywise has been drawn to this cruelty, violence, and impending death, called there by the actions of the attackers themselves rather than serving as an active agent in their assault of Adrian, particularly since Pennywise usually preys upon children, influencing but rarely feeding on adults.[29]

Much the same could be argued of the scene that precedes Bev's abduction in *IT Chapter One*. Bev's abuse is well established at this point in the narrative, but this time she defies her father and his response is swift, physical, and violent. Both Bev's refusal and her father's assault are a notable contrast to the preceding scenes of abuse, where she has passively submitted to him touching her and stroking her hair. This time, his attack is aggressive and explosive, though Bev matches him in her self-defense, escapes, and knocks him out only to find herself in Pennywise's grip when she turns away from her unconscious father. Just as with Adrian's murder, there is uncertainty about the cause-and-effect relationship of this violent interaction: the shift in Bev's father's may have been It's influence taking over or could simply have been the culmination of his own violent impulses. Pennywise could be waiting just behind Bev in the apartment bathroom because It vacated its control of Bev's father when she knocked him unconscious or because It sensed and was attracted to the violence. Regardless of the specific lines of influence, the relationship between It and the people of Derry is symbiotic and destructive. The people of Derry may look the other way, ignoring the horrific things that happen in their town, or they may be sources of horror themselves, in the terror, abuse, and violence they inflict upon others.

Derry, It, and the horrors of which Derry's residents are capable are inseparable. It's influence is foundational to Derry's identity, infused in every element of the town, its history, and its people. Muschietti foregrounds the importance of place, providing viewers with a sense of familiarity and an intimate knowledge of Derry that, in effect, makes Derry a character in its own right, with the town as a whole choosing to look the other way, ignore its past and present violence, and provide a home and hunting ground for Pennywise.

Notes

1. James Arthur Anderson, *The Linguistics of Stephen King: Layered Language and Meaning in the Fiction* (Jefferson, NC: McFarland & Company, 2017), 122.
2. Anderson, 122.
3. The significance of these key locations and the connection between characters and specific places is visually and narratively underscored in the design of the board game *IT: Evil Below*, in which each of the seven members of the Losers' Club is associated with locations in Derry, including Bill with the House on Neibolt Street, Ben with the Barrens, Stan with the Standpipe, Mike with Quality Meats Butcher Shop, Bev with her apartment, Richie with the Town Square, and Eddie with Keene's Pharmacy. This is also an example of the intertextual engagement between multiple versions of the narrative: while Stan has horrific experiences at the Standpipe in both King's novel and in Wallace's miniseries, he does not have a strong association with this location in Muschietti's films, in which the Standpipe largely serves as a recognizable Derry landmark rather than a narratively significant source of horror, appearing on the postcard on which Ben writes his anonymous poem to Bev and in the background as Bill waits for Bev to meet him.
4. Anderson, 122.
5. Stephen King, *Danse Macabre* (New York: Gallery, 2010 [1981]), 278.
6. King, *Danse Macabre*, 279.

7. Quoted in Josh Wigler, "'Castle Rock': How Hulu's Stephen King Anthology Series Was Born," *Hollywood Reporter*, 25 July 2018, https://www.hollywoodreporter.com/live-feed/castle-rock-series-premiere-stephen-king-hulu-series-explained-1129538. Thomason was one of the show-runners of the Hulu original series *Castle Rock* (2018–2019), which similarly explores how an entire town can be filled with inexplicable mysteries and horrors. *Castle Rock* draws on King's fiction, including familiar characters like Alan Pangborn and iconic locations like Shawshank State Prison, but creates a new slate of interconnected characters and narratives. The first season of *Castle Rock* centers on a mysterious figure called The Kid, who has been discovered locked in a cage in the depths of Shawshank, played by Bill Skarsgård. This casting choice, coupled with The Kid's 27-year imprisonment, his ability to influence others, and his seemingly ageless nature, led some fans to speculate that there may be metaverse connections between *IT* and *Castle Rock* (Romain), though upon closer consideration of *Castle Rock*'s narrative and the inhuman nature of the monster in *IT*, this does not seem likely. Chosen Jacobs also appears in both, as young Mike Hanlon in *IT* and as Wendell Deaver in *Castle Rock*.

8. Peter Larkin Romaneski, *The Gothic Place as the Center of Power and Ruin* (Masters Thesis), Florida State University, 2009, http://www.diginole.lib.fsu.edu/islandora/object/fsu%3A176315.

9. A.O. Scott, "Review: 'It' Brings Back Stephen King's Killer Clown," *The New York Times*, 6 Sept. 2017, https://www.nytimes.com/2017/09/06/movies/it-review-stephen-king.html.

10. Physical and sexual abuse can be included in this list as well, though much of that happens within the domestic space and behind closed doors, while the abuse and marginalization addressed here occur in public spaces. The abuse Bev suffers at the hands of her father is addressed at length in Chapters 4 and 5.

11. Joey Warren, "LGBTQ+ Representation in Horror," *The Current*, 11 Feb. 2020, https://www.thecurrentmsu.com/2020/02/12/lgbtq-representation-in-horror/.

12. Iman Jaroudi, "Horrific Homophobia: Queer (Mis)Representation in Horror," *Broad Recognition*, 29 Oct. 2020, https://www.broadsatyale.com/queer-misrepresentation-in-horror/.

13. Emily Burnham, "The 1984 Murder of Charlie Howard in Bangor Will Be Dramatized in the 'IT' Sequel," *Bangor Daily News*. 4 Sept. 2019, https://www.bangordailynews.com/2019/09/04/news/bangor/the-1984-murder-of-charlie-howard-in-bangor-will-be-dramatized-in-the-it-sequel/. Like Adrian, Howard had asthma; Howard "drowned in three feet of water" (Wax, 22) after being beaten and thrown off the bridge by his attackers.

14. Quoted in David Crow, "It Chapter Two: Adrian Mellon and Derry Hate Crimes," *Den of*

Geek, 19 July 2019, https://www.denofgeek.com/movies/it-chapter-two-adrian-mellon-derry-hate-crimes/.

15. Eddie briefly mentions the AIDS epidemic in his panic over whether or not it is safe for them to care for Ben following his attack by Bowers, including panicked misunderstandings about transmission through contact with a dirty subway pole and his fear that the alley might be full of discarded needles (*IT Chapter One*). This fear also informs his nightmare experience in the basement of Keene's Pharmacy, which is filled with used needles and bags of blood (*IT Chapter Two*).

16. Southern Poverty Law Center, "The Year in Hate and Extremism 2019: A Report from the Southern Poverty Law Center," *Southern Poverty Law Center*, 2019, https://www.splcenter.org/sites/default/files/yih_2020_final.pdf.

17. Tony Magistrale, *Landscape of Fear: Stephen King's American Gothic* (Madison: University of Wisconsin Press, 1988), 111.

18. Representations of the Shokopiwah, their role within the narrative of *IT Chapter Two*, and the Ritual of Chüd are discussed further in Chapters 3 and 5.

19. John Sears, *Stephen King's Gothic* (Gothic Literary Studies) (Cardiff: University of Wales Press, 2011), 156.

20. Sears, 156.

21. The adults themselves may not be wholly aware of the show either, which appears on the televisions when they are largely unengaged, with Bev's father out of the room and Henry's father sleeping in front of the television, suggesting a potentially subconscious influence. There seems to be a sense of agency at work as well and, when Bev's father prepares to reenter the living room, an in-progress baseball game is audible on the television rather than the *Derry Children's Hour*.

22. Brian W. Smith, "The Clown Will Eat You Now," *The Many Lives of IT: Essays on the Stephen King Horror Franchise*, edited by Ron Riekki (Jefferson, NC: McFarland, 2020), 185.

23. Smith, 185.

24. Smith, 185. Scott Wampler ("You Might've Missed One of IT's Best Scares," *Birth. Movies. Death.*, 10 Sept. 2017, https://www.birthmoviesdeath.com/2017/09/10/you-might-have-missed-one-of-its-best-scares) provides a close reading of this scene and the significance of the old woman specifically, noting that while they are visually coded as two different women, the old woman who watches Ben "may well be a double of the librarian, who we see across the room in a later shot. And if that's the case ... well, [then] it wasn't the librarian who gave Ben that book, was it?"

25. Wampler.

26. Deleted scenes in the special features of *IT Chapter One* further emphasize this abuse, showing the welts and bruises on Henry's back where his father has beaten him, likely with a belt. The special features also include an extended scene of Henry waiting outside the house on Neibolt Street before attacking the Losers, with the bodies of his friends Belch Huggins (Jake Sim) and Victor Chris (Logan Thompson), who he also murdered after killing his father. A still image of this deleted scene is also included in Wax (184).

27. Magistrale, *Landscape of Fear*, 112.

28. Lunman's dual roles in Muschietti's films, as Betty Ripsom and Chris Unwin, are particularly interesting as Lunman plays both victim and villain, each of whom are horrifying in their own right, as well as effectively playing characters of different gender identities, with the female Ripsom and male Unwin.

29. Notably, Mike does include Adrian's murder in the new cycle of violence he lays out for his fellow Losers, indicating a connection, whether active or passive, in the larger narrative of Pennywise's violence and the Losers' return (*IT Chapter Two*).

Chapter 3: Pennywise the Dancing Clown

While the monster in *IT* takes on a variety of forms—a leper, a headless child, and an enormous spider creature, among others—its most frequent and iconic face is that of Pennywise the Dancing Clown. Clowns have long been seen as unsettling, with the painted face belying the potentially dark reality beneath. While the clown has been a long-established figure within the horror tradition, it is particularly ubiquitous in the horror boom of the 2010s, with the appearance of Twisty the Clown in *American Horror Story: Freak Show* (2015), Rob Zombie's *31* (2016), and a new iteration of Gotham City's infamous *Joker* (2019) with the anarchic clown played by Joaquin Phoenix.[1] Paralleling the on-screen resurgence of scary clowns, there was also the "clown panic" of 2016, with mysterious and menacing figures dressed as clowns and prowling the streets in France, England, and America, with explanations ranging from pranks and publicity stunts to experimental film projects.

While often nostalgically framed as playful figures of an idealized past, clowns have always been complicated characters that evoke both laughter and anxiety. In his 2016 book *Bad Clowns*, Benjamin Radford combines history, folklore, and popular culture to critically consider the figure of the bad clown. Radford argues:

> It's a fallacy to ask when clowns went bad, because they were never really good … From a historic, folkloric perspective, they were always ambiguous, trickster figures: the early versions of the clown are court jesters, the harlequin of *commedia dell'arte*, Mr. Punch. Sometimes they were funny, sometimes they were horrific. The evil side of the clown character was always there.[2]

These clowns were figures of subversion, with the court jester able to mock monarchs and Mr Punch acting with unrestrained and unpunished violence, operating outside the status quo, unpredictable and uncontrollable.

The clown also exists in overlapping spaces of humor and horror, a position of uncertainty and liminality. In "Horror and Humor," Noël Carroll argues that, while these two approaches may seem counterintuitive and mutually exclusive, "There is some intimate relation of affinity between horror and humor,"[3] interrogating the ways in which both the horrific and the humorous surprise their reader or viewer, catch them off guard. Carroll identifies the clown as "a monster ... Not only are clowns exaggeratedly misshapen and, at times, outright travesties of the human form—contortions played on our paradigms of the human shape—they also possess a physical resiliency conjoined with muscular and cognitive dysfunctionalities that mark them off as an imaginary species."[4] Through this exaggerated performance, the clown is able to achieve physical feats, contort his body, and bounce back from physical abuse in ways that transcend the limitations of the human form.[5] Expectation and the perception of danger are often the determining factor between horror and humor: whether or not the figure in question is perceived as a threat. As Carroll explains, "Fear must be directed at something that is perceived to be or believed to be harmful. Standardly, one cannot be afraid of something that one does not believe is harmful."[6] As has already been established by the example of Mr Punch and others, clowns are masters of misrule, uncontrollable and uncontainable; as a result, they are always potentially threatening, even if that "threat" is as innocuous as being made the butt of a clown's joke or an unwitting figure in his charade.

In their painting and parody of the human face, clowns are also uncanny, which Sigmund Freud outlined as that which is simultaneously familiar and alien, a dissonance that mires the individual in the realm of "intellectual uncertainty."[7] With their painted faces, exaggerated bodies that often sport oversized feet or cartoony white-gloved hands, and acrobatic antics, Mark Dery argues that clowns are constantly "vacillating disconcertingly between human and nonhuman, animate and inanimate."[8] This combination of subversion and the uncanny make the clown an inherently unsettling figure because this means the audience has no way of knowing who (or what) he is and what he will do next. The clown may do handsprings or present a whimsical balloon animal, but he could just as easily hit the viewer in the face with a pie or a violent spray of water. When faced with a clown, the threat of humiliation and perhaps even pain is never off the table.

John Wayne Gacy's history of clowning has become a real-life cultural touchstone for the potential for violence and a dark intent lurking behind the painted face. A serial killer who tortured, sexually assaulted, and murdered at least 33 young men in the greater Chicago area in the 1970s, Gacy's disguise was two-fold: the first as a "friendly, hard-working guy" and the second as Pogo the Clown.[9] Gacy reveled in the freedom he was able to enjoy as a clown, insulting and even groping bystanders along parade routes, later telling police that as a clown "you can get away with a lot of things ... A clown can get away with murder."[10] Though Gacy did not dress as a clown when he lured, abused, or murdered his victims, the duality of appearance and reality was still unsettlingly prescient, in "the chilling moment when Gacy morphed from a gregarious big brother, clowning around with his young victim, into a pitiless psychopath who could pause, in the midst of strangling someone, to chat nonchalantly on the phone."[11] Throughout his trial, Gacy was dubbed the "Killer Clown," sensationalizing and foregrounding the unknowability and potential danger that could be lurking behind the greasepainted smile, resituating the threat from entertainment and fantasy to a potentially fatal reality.

This sense of real-life danger and uncertainty was further amplified by the clown hysteria of 1981, with rumors of clowns lurking around schools and parks, which occurred simultaneous with a range of other fears that threatened children specifically, including "new fears of child kidnappings and the panic surrounding a wave of false accusations of satanic ritual abuse in day cares throughout the nation ... [As] The country's repressed anxieties found their outlet in the specter of psychotic clowns and the unknown occult."[12] Building on the uncanny danger of the clown figure throughout history, Gacy's infamy and the high-profile hysteria surrounding the 1981 clown sightings were likely on the minds of readers—and perhaps even King himself—when they came face-to-(painted) face with Pennywise in King's 1986 novel.

These clown panics also seem to be cyclical, with the 2013 appearance of England's Northampton Clown and the more widespread 2016 clown sightings making headlines in the years before Muschietti's films. This repetition echoes the return of the monster Itself, as Matthew Dessem notes that "Pennywise appearances come in waves—much like the 1981, 1991, and 2016 clusters of evil clown sightings."[13] This correlation is inexact and coincidental, though it does point to a larger truth: whether it is a rash of scary clown sightings or Pennywise himself, when it comes to fear of the unknown and the uncanny, the horror may fade but it is never truly defeated and it always comes back.

PENNYWISE AND THE UNCANNY

Like the cadre of scary clowns that have come before, Pennywise blurs the lines between horror and humor, reveling in the appeal of the uncanny to attract, disarm, and terrorize his victims. In his consideration of the uncanny and how humans respond to that amorphous feeling of being "creeped out," psychologist Frank T. McAndrew addresses this indefinable fear and the potential danger of ignoring this feeling. As he explains the impulse of polite and appropriate interaction:

> It would be considered rude and strange to run away in the middle of a conversation with someone who is sending out a creepy vibe but is actually harmless; at the same time, it could be perilous to ignore your intuition and engage with that individual if he is, in fact, a threat. The ambivalence leaves you frozen in place, wallowing in discomfort.[14]

This dissonance, as well as the anxiety and potential danger it provokes, was central to Muschietti's determination of Pennywise's look and mannerisms. As the director points out, "The appearance of Pennywise is at the same time intriguing and alluring … There's something wrong with him, but it's also shrouded in some sort of magic that is quite unsettling."[15] This uncertainty and a sense of childlike curiosity are central to Pennywise's appeal to his youngest victims specifically: Georgie Denbrough in *IT Chapter One* and Victoria Fuller in *IT Chapter Two*.

Georgie is Pennywise's first victim of It's new cycle and, from the moment he sees the clown peering up at him from the storm drain, Georgie is uncertain, torn between curiosity, an innate sense of unease, and the well-learned lesson of the danger of talking to strangers. The camera angles in the shot–reverse shot conversation between Georgie and Pennywise place Georgie in the dominant position, with low-angle shots featuring Georgie's face and high-angle shots looking down at Pennywise, but the combination of danger and curiosity belie this visual establishment of power or control, starting with the moment Pennywise opens his eyes unexpectedly in the darkness of the storm drain and then as he keeps his face partially concealed in shadows as their conversation continues. This also puts the viewer in Georgie's position, leaning over and looking down, as the camera moves from the street view to a closeup of Pennywise's unsettling face. As Michelle Leigh Gompf notes:

When he talks to Georgie, he is looking up from the sewer, but mostly with his eyes. He does not tilt his head up. It is a submissive look, a pleading look, which further emphasizes the whites of his eyes. His eyes don't seem to blink and his stare is intense, but not frighteningly so, due to the continued small smile, which reveals only a glimpse of the white of his teeth.[16]

While Georgie's first instinct is to jump back from the sewer and ostensibly to safety, Pennywise subverts the young boy's expectations by engaging him in polite conversation, complimenting his paper boat and speaking matter-of-factly with no acknowledgement at all that he stands in a space which should not be possible, remaining dry and unmoved despite the swiftly flowing water. Gompf argues that the dissonance in this interaction makes Pennywise "more intriguing than a contemporary circus clown. With a contemporary circus clown there are the questions: How'd he get in the sewer? Why is he there? ... [With] Pennywise, the questions become: Do I really see what I think I see? Is he a clown or something else?"[17] Georgie is temporarily paralyzed by this uncertainty and ambivalence, unable to simply walk—or run screaming—away from the unsettling face of a clown in the sewer. Pennywise works to allay Georgie's fears, at least in part, with descriptions of the circus and the popping of the popcorn; Georgie lets his guard down, "popping" and giggling along, comforted by this hilarity, though this ease is thrown off-balance once more when Pennywise lapses into a dead-eyed stasis mid-pop. Pennywise's fixed gaze, off-kilter eyes, and drooling lips similarly belie the easy banter he engages in with Georgie, keeping Georgie in a state of tension between amusement and terror, his uncertainty anchoring him before Pennywise. When fear and unease win out and Georgie is poised to leave, it is a different kind of fear that keeps him moored one tragic moment longer, in his thoughts of Bill's disappointment at his younger brother's loss of the *S.S. Georgie*. While Georgie's anguished "Bill's gonna kill me" (*IT Chapter One*) as the boat shot away from him was hyperbole, when Pennywise repeats these words in his deadpan delivery, they become a threat and, while Georgie certainly knows that his big brother would never really hurt him, Georgie's love for Bill and his fear of disappointing him are enough to make him reach out to take his boat back, even though every other instinct is telling him to run.

Victoria Fuller in *IT Chapter Two* is similarly unarmed and drawn in by her curiosity though, in her case, this response is amplified by kindness as Pennywise plays on the young girl's sympathy. Victoria is immediately on guard, poised to walk away before their conversation has even properly begun, rejecting Pennywise's introduction and offer of friendship, asking "If you're my friend, why are you hiding in the dark?" (*IT Chapter Two*). While Pennywise remains largely hidden in the shadows, much like in his first encounter with Georgie—and the audience's introduction to this iconic villain—in contrast to Georgie's high-angle perspective, Victoria's view is head on, as Pennywise stands crouched, putting them on an even level. Victoria initially rejects McAndrew's state of ambivalence, trusting her instinct and prepared to flee. However, where curiosity has failed, empathy succeeds and Pennywise's tears as she walks away achieve the connection he seeks. Victoria may be too savvy to trust this unsettling stranger, but she is all too familiar with being teased for her appearance, made fun of for the strawberry birthmark on her cheek, and Pennywise's promise that he can easily rid her of it is an offer too tempting to refuse. Georgie's terror of disappointing Bill held him in It's thrall and here, Victoria's longing for acceptance does the same, as she walks willingly into danger, intentionally ignoring the warning signs that had so recently put her on alert. Both Georgie and Victoria find themselves trapped in McAndrew's state of ambiguity, drawn on by a combination of childlike curiosity and their own insecurities, which are exploited and manipulated by Pennywise to keep these two children in a state of paralysis between their expectations of normality and the monstrously horrific reality before them, enabling It to feed on both their bodies and their fear.

Much of the horror of clowns comes from seeing them in places they do not belong. Lon Chaney famously pointed out the importance of context and dissonance with his observation: "A clown is funny in the circus ring, but what would be the normal reaction to opening a door at midnight and finding the same clown there in the moonlight?"[18] *IT Chapter One* and *Chapter Two* are full of moments where the clown appears in places where it really should not be, like the sewers, an abandoned house, and under the bleachers at a baseball game. However, Pennywise and other variations on the clown figure also show up in places where their appearance would be expected or even natural with no less terror, including celebrations in the town square in *IT Chapter One* and the festival funhouse in *IT Chapter Two*. In *IT Chapter One*, when the young Losers are comparing notes in the park, there is a clown on the bandstand stage entertaining children, seemingly innocuous and unthreatening. Richie here notes his professed fear of clowns as the clown extends a balloon animal towards him. The clown's awareness and acknowledgement of the Losers suggests that this is likely Pennywise in disguise, a dangerous threat in clear and public view, though the park full of people—including the multiple police officers who pass through the background of the Losers' conversation—remain oblivious.

In the Derry Canal Days Festival funhouse, Pennywise similarly appears in an expected context, one clown among many, though his presence here—as elsewhere—proves horrific. As Bill pursues Dean through the festival in an attempt to save the boy, he enters the funhouse itself through the mouth of a giant clown and then has to dodge a series of brightly colored swinging clowns as he makes his way down a corridor of blacklights and optical illusions, before entering the mirror maze at the heart of the funhouse. The funhouse as a whole is designed to manipulate the individual's perceptions, including the striped barrel Bill must pass through as the world outside is literally turned upside down—in a visual echo of the camera angle's rotating emergence from the tunnel of the culvert pipe following the opening scene of *IT Chapter One*— marking Bill's transition from the world outside into the liminal and carnivalesque space of the funhouse, where all perception is suspect. Though Bill times and dodges the swaying clowns fairly effectively, this does not stop him from being taken out by one, knocked into the wall and off his balance, both physically and emotionally, as his terror threatens to overwhelm him. This skewed perception is naturally amplified by the mirror maze, with flashing lights, corridors that shrink, chambers that alternate between darkness and light, seemingly open passages that abruptly dead-end, and reflections that multiply and disorient. While Bill struggles in his pursuit of Dean, Pennywise is able to effortlessly move through these barriers, scuttling easily across a passage Bill has just vacated. The funhouse itself also takes on a more sinister geography under Pennywise's influence, as Dean finds himself trapped in a glass box and unable to escape, powerless as Pennywise and Bill work from opposite sides to break through the glass and get to the boy. While all other sides of the mirror maze feature a backdrop of more mirrors, Pennywise stands in front of a red curtain, further emphasizing the performative nature of this particular attack, intended specifically for Bill to see, though he is powerless to stop it. After Pennywise has devoured Dean, the form of the mirror maze stabilizes, with the wall before Bill becoming an unchanging mirror once more, concealing the horrific scene he has just witnessed.

Figure 6. The inversion of the funhouse tunnel

Even when Pennywise himself is not present or posing an immediate threat, his influence is pervasive and he appears in the background, transcending time, place, and context. Pennywise is shown in the crowd scene of one of the old Derry images on Ben's bedroom wall and his face peers out from the peeling paint of the mural in the alley outside the butcher shop (*IT Chapter One*). Even when the Losers have escaped Derry, Pennywise remains present in their lives and his face appears in the background of a painting of Bev and her husband Tom (Will Beinbrink), briefly visible on the landing of their home as she flees from Tom's abuse (*IT Chapter Two*).[19] While these appearances are less overtly foregrounded, Pennywise's constant presence in the background of the Losers' lives and the larger history of Derry is clearly established, demonstrating the way in which horror can hide in plain sight, undetected but still dangerous.

PENNYWISE IN PAST AND PRESENT

A clown's makeup and costume design are distinctive, a mark of their individuality and one that is fiercely defended. As Dave Fagundes and Aaron Perzanowski note: "there's consensus among clowns about the importance of not copying one another,"[20] a code

IT CHAPTERS ONE AND TWO

that is maintained and strictly enforced within the clown community. This dedication to a personalized aesthetic is reflected in the very different looks of the on-screen iterations of Pennywise: Tim Curry's iconic performance in Wallace's 1990 miniseries and Bill Skarsgård in Muschietti's *IT Chapter One* and *Chapter Two*. In addition to reflecting this larger tradition of unique self-fashioning within the clowning community, Curry and Skarsgård's respective appearances are also significant features in the different approaches to horror each director mobilizes.

In his first description of Pennywise in King's novel, the author draws on the imagery of well-established clown figures, as Georgie notes that the clown "looked like a cross between Bozo and [*Howdy Doody*'s] Clarabell ... The face of the clown in the stormdrain was white, there were funny tufts of red hair on either side of his bald head, and there was a big clown-smile painted over his mouth."[21] Just as the clown itself is a harbinger of the uncanny—simultaneously recognizable and strange—so is Georgie's first impression of Pennywise. The young boy is able to define what he is looking at (a clown), though not why it should be where he has found it (in a sewer in the midst of a historic flood). Similarly, while Georgie is unsettled and on guard, he is also entranced, associating the figure he sees before him with fun and happy memories, like laughing at *The Howdy Doody Show*. When in his final moments Georgie glimpses the monster that lurks beneath It's clown mask, what he sees is impossible to articulate or survive, as "what he saw destroyed his sanity in one clawing stroke."[22] Both Wallace and Muschietti had to contend with not only the face of Pennywise—though this is the one It wears most often—but with how to visualize that which lies beneath as well.

Tim Curry's Pennywise draws on the iconography of the classic clown, with his baggy, brightly colored costume with big orange pom-pom buttons and a smooth white-painted face. Topped with a horseshoe of voluminous red hair and a round red nose, Curry's Pennywise is recognizable, reminiscent of a clown one might glimpse at a circus or walking down the street accompanying a parade. He jumps enthusiastically about, twirls a noisemaker, and, at times, holds a large bunch of multicolored balloons in one white-gloved hand. His lips are naturalistically painted, rather than the exaggerated smile or grimace of iconic clowns like Bozo, amplifying his straight-faced deadpan expression and making the contortions of his laughter and his snarls simultaneously horrifying and human in appearance. This familiar design also corresponds with the fun embodied by Pennywise in his manic moments, a comedic sensibility through which Curry "brought a completely obnoxious, loud, unhinged sense of humor to the character,"[23] though the menace and potential for violence never lurk far beneath the surface. With the limited special effects budget and other restrictions of primetime network television, Pennywise's monstrous transformations were restrained in Wallace's miniseries, with the most memorable effect being a bulging mouth full of fangs as It devours Georgie and later taunts and torments the Losers Club. Curry's Pennywise quickly became iconic, making comparisons inevitable with the costuming and performance of Skarsgård's Pennywise in Muschietti's *IT* films.

While Curry's Pennywise costuming draws on recognizable elements of twentieth-century clowns, for Muschietti's films, costume designer Janie Bryant looked further back, incorporating visual elements and design details from "images of Victorian clowns and acrobats,"[24] though there are elements of other time periods reflected in Pennywise's costume as well, including the Medieval, Renaissance, and Elizabethan eras.[25] This historical grounding lends itself to a more subdued color palette than that of the contemporary clown, with shades of ivory, gray, and muted colors, like the dull orange of Pennywise's pom-pom buttons. This inspiration drawn from of a range of past eras also reflects Pennywise's own timeless nature and Bryant notes: "The costume definitely incorporates all these otherworldly past lives, if you will. He is definitely a clown from a different time."[26] In addition to establishing the larger context of Pennywise's long and destructive life, this firm grounding in history also harks back to the darker and more serious role of clowns, as disrupters of order and challengers of the status quo within the larger scope of established, firmly grounded structures that often left ordinary citizens powerless and vulnerable to exploitation. With these class disparities underlying the role of clowns and court jesters in Medieval times, these performances were "a sanctioned way for people under the feudal thumb to laugh at the guys in charge."[27] Rather than entertaining audiences with an amusing dance or by crafting a balloon animal, these clowns' humor had the potential to be cutting, subversive, and even, potentially, revolutionary. Though these antics were more of a release valve than a call to arms or instigator of any real change, part of their purpose was to challenge power and reveal the truth beneath the façade, which is an inherently unsettling proposition and highlights the dynamics and disparities between those in power and the powerless, a distinction that resonates in Muschietti's films as well, not just in Pennywise's interactions with the Losers Club, but in the marginalized position of children in general as they navigate their way through the conventions and expectations of a world run by their parents and other adults. This position of powerlessness is further amplified by the exclusion these particular children face, as they are harassed and bullied by their peers as well, including the physical threat of Henry and the more emotional abuse leveled by Gretta.

The muted color scheme of Pennywise's costume also enables him to lurk in the background, to blend in with shadows and perhaps even become one himself. As a result, It's presence is more insidious in Muschietti's films. The more modern costume of Curry's Pennywise announces itself, drawing the eye and irrefutably marking something out of the ordinary (even when the specific danger is not immediately apparent). It is neither subtle nor sneaky. The costume of the contemporary clown is a conspicuous spectacle, intended to be seen and looked at, examined and critiqued. As Smith argues, this costuming and physicality are central to the characterization of each Pennywise, as "Curry's interpretation comes across like simply a man in a clown suit that occasionally bares his fangs to scare his prey ... [while] Skarsgård's Pennywise is an otherworldly being wearing the guise of a human that is, in turn, wearing a clown suit."[28] As a result, the ways in which Skarsgård's Pennywise moves through and interacts with the world around him, as well as with the children upon whom he preys, is more nuanced and diffuse. The grays and dingy whites of Skarsgård's Pennywise do not announce themselves so brashly, as It lurks in the shadows, watching and waiting, manipulating the people and horrors that surround It. The brightest element of Muschietti's Pennywise is his red balloon which, whether singly or great bunches, announces It's presence and influence, even when Pennywise is nowhere to be seen, as in the message It leaves for Mike under the bridge following the murder of Adrian Mellon that grounds *IT Chapter Two* in the present moment.

Skarsgård's Pennywise is able to come and go with little fanfare, seeming to appear out of nowhere, emerging from the shadows, and then disappearing again with similar ease, with his costuming and appearance visually echoing "Pennywise's ability to fade into and out of his surroundings,"[29] ephemeral, uncontainable, and "floating."[30] While Curry's Pennywise dramatically pops in and out, with clear bookending moments of when the horror begins and ends in his antagonizing of the Losers Club, the presence of Skarsgård's Pennywise is less clearly demarcated. It's potential presence is a constant, sinister possibility, even when the Losers think they are alone, either individually or with one another, as in Pennywise's gradual emergence from Bill's projected slideshow of family vacation photos or when Ben hides in his locker, believing himself alone and safe, only to have Pennywise's contorted face emerge from the shadows just over his shoulder. It separates itself from these blurred images and shadows, and is similarly able to melt back into them and disappear just as easily in an unnerving cycle of absence, presence, and absence once more, subsumed again in the larger Derry—including its inhabitants' personal and interpersonal nightmares—of which It is such an integral part.

The fitted silhouette of Pennywise's costume also accentuates the sharpness and explosive nature of his movements, which lack the rolling fluidity of more traditionally acrobatic clowns, as well as the dominating physical presence of Skarsgård's 6'4" frame, which is particularly accentuated as he towers over and menaces the children. His movements are simultaneously graceful and violent, with the fitted nature of his costume emphasizing these dissonant physical characteristics, such as when he frenetically charges to attack Bill in the flooded basement before passively melting back off of the stairs into the darkness below in *IT Chapter One* or when he floats serenely down from the Paul Bunyan statue in the town square in *IT Chapter Two*, arms and legs akimbo as he taunts and threatens Richie.

Figure 7. Pennywise's costuming and physicality

An illustrative example of Pennywise's physical explosiveness is Richie Tozier's childhood encounter with Pennywise in the house on Neibolt Street. After discovering a poster that proclaims him to be one of the missing kids, Richie is separated and isolated from his friends, discovering a room lined with clown figures (including an homage to Curry's Pennywise) and an aisle that leads to a coffin occupied by a jointed-doll version of his own dead body. Richie closes the coffin lid in rejection and disgust, only to have it spring back open with Pennywise's explosive release, as he flies with limbs extended high into the air before landing on the once again closed coffin lid. Combining a classic jump scare with the imagery of a monstrous jack-in-the-box, Pennywise's body is showcased in a low-angle shot, clearly defined as one of agility, power, and danger, with his presence outlined and underscored by the cut and design of his costume, rather than being enveloped and shrouded in a baggy, traditional clown suit. As he comes to land on the top of the coffin, visual equilibrium is reestablished, once again positioning the viewer with the victim's point of view, as Richie looks on in horror, first at Pennywise's crouched body, poised to spring again, then zooming in to feature a closeup of the clown's face. Bryant explains the rationale and design aesthetic of the costume's fit with an intent of "accentuat[ing] the unique, childish, puppet-like movement"[31] of Skarsgård's performance, with the sharpness and detail of these movements central to his surprise attack on Richie.

The puppet imagery Bryant describes is particularly significant as well, with Richie discovering a doll version of himself within the coffin, as ranks of clown figures look on, with one even turning its wooden head to track Richie's passage with its painted, unblinking eyes. This scene collapses the spaces between It and Richie in dramatic fashion, bringing Richie face-to-face with Pennywise, and with the realization of his own mortality, as under his humor and bravado Richie realizes that he could easily be one of the missing kids, becoming nearly hysterical at the sight of the poster bearing his face. Additionally, despite his professed fear of clowns, while Richie is understandably unsettled by the clown figures he encounters here, he is not paralyzed by fear, even tapping one on the face and dismissing them as "Stupid clowns" (*IT Chapter One*) as he makes his way to the coffin, which holds the bulk of his attention and seems to be his main source of fear and curiosity. This could indicate competing fears—the realization of one's own potential death is likely to take precedence over many other stimuli—but it is just as likely that Richie's averred fear of clowns was a glib, throwaway response, designed to appease his friends while keeping his truest fears and deepest secrets to himself. If this is the case, Richie's act of deception is mirrored in the figure of the clown itself, a painted face and outward appearance that belies the reality concealed beneath.

Another moment of horror that emphasizes the fitted nature of Pennywise's suit and the contours and danger of his body beneath also occurs during the young Losers' visit to the house on Neibolt Street. While Pennywise's airborne leap from Richie's coffin foregrounds the acrobatics often associated with clowns, when he emerges from the Neibolt Street house refrigerator, it is not as an acrobat but as a contortionist. As Eddie cradles his broken arm, he first sees Pennywise's white-gloved hand emerge from behind the refrigerator door, playfully drumming his fingers as he waits to be noticed, before opening the door to reveal his twisted body within. Following the foundational uncanniness of clowns, what Eddie sees filling the refrigerator is horrifying in both its recognizability and in its wrongness: the bends and angles of Pennywise's body, the head and hands at the bottom as the rest of him unfurls, emphasized by the increasingly low-angle position of the shot as Pennywise rises to full height, followed by his torso untwisting and head reversing position to face forward before Pennywise begins to advance upon Eddie.

Just as with the parallels between the puppet qualities of Pennywise's movements and the doll-like version of Richie laid in the coffin, in this scene both Pennywise and Eddie display bodies that should not be bent and twisted the way they are, in Eddie's broken arm and the unnatural collapsing—and subsequent readjustment—of Pennywise's body within the abandoned house's refrigerator. In these two encounters, the monstrous and the human are brought into alignment with one another, with both Richie and Eddie frozen by fear and isolated from their friends by It's destructive influence and their interactions with Pennywise as he taunts and torments them, in this case advancing on Eddie with herky-jerky movements, an exaggerated crying face, and snapping bites from a low-angle camera position as he looms over Eddie, before being stopped in his tracks by the arrival of Bill and Richie. In both cases Richie and Eddie are enveloped by and implicated in the bodily difference enacted by Pennywise, but in contrast to the performative nature of the clown, who can take hits and falls only to spring back unscathed, the boys' human nature is reasserted, with Richie reclaiming his agency and

Eddie's broken arm having serious consequences both for him individually and for the collective dynamic of the Losers Club.

One final illustrative example that demonstrates Pennywise's performance and subversion of the physicality of the clown is in the brief dance he performs in the cistern where It has taken Bev in *IT Chapter One*. This is the most overtly performative of his clowning actions, with the circus wagon serving as both backdrop and stage, accompanied by the personalized call to "Step right up, Beverly!" and festive circus music. While the tropes and traditions are familiar ones—the carnival barking, the pyrotechnics of the sparklers as the wagon opens, the music—they are immediately revealed as a dark parody. As Pennywise's stage is revealed, it is filled not with bright streamers or other circus imagery, but is instead a multilayered backdrop of fringe, fire, and "billowing apocalyptic clouds,"[32] a scene of infernal destruction rather than playful fun. Pennywise is showcased with a wide-angle shot, emphasizing his dancing form and his circus wagon stage, though the camera quickly moves closer, zooming in with a juddering camera movement to zero in on his face. While Pennywise frequently smiles, whether in an attempt to put his potential victims at ease or in a display of monstrosity, his familiar grin is here notably missing, replaced instead by a frowning grimace as he launches into a spirited dance. The exaggerated movement of Pennywise's arms and legs echo their wide, cartoonish swings as he advanced on Eddie in the house on Neibolt Street. As Pennywise dances on the makeshift stage of the circus wagon, his movements are stiff and mechanical, energetic but with a sense of the predetermined, like those of a mechanical doll; even his eyes remain unfocused, looking at some indeterminate point in front of and above himself rather than directly at Beverly. When Beverly gauges her odds and decides to make a run for it, however, Pennywise springs once more to aware and explosive life, leaping in a spread-eagled pounce from the stage to cut off her escape route, easily catching and lifting her with a single hand—with the visual dynamics inverted once more, echoing Georgie's death as Pennywise's face is shown from a high-angle position that mimics Bev's own perspective—effortlessly demonstrating his speed, strength, and agility.

The clown is also not It's true form and Pennywise's costuming in *IT Chapter One* and *Chapter Two* alludes to this darker reality as well, as "Every part of the costume aims to suggest something ancient and evoke something disturbing."[33] While It takes on a wide range of forms over the course of the films, one that refers specifically back to King's novel and Wallace's 1990 miniseries is that of an enormous spider. While this spider form plays a significantly smaller role in Muschietti's film, it inspired Bryant to incorporate an organic aesthetic in some elements of the Pennywise costume, with the stiffness of his jacket in particular "creating a quality akin to an exoskeleton."[34] Bryant also "added pleats in the jacket, sleeves and legs to give Pennywise, as she says, 'that organic, caterpillar, creepy feel,'" while the frayed edges of Pennywise's collar evoke the imagery of a spider web.[35] Marjorie Galas notes that, "The back also has a pleated spine that further replicated a reptilian movement,"[36] an effect that is highlighted by Pennywise in motion, which is an often insectile combination of stiffness and fluidity. Pennywise's movement is organic, though distinctly not human, at times echoing the physical presence and vertebral motion of the H.R. Giger-designed xenomorph from Ridley Scott's *Alien* (1979) as Pennywise rises to stand or turns to attack. This sharp angularity and exoskeletal design is also highlighted in the vision that Mike shares with Bill, in It's form as a monstrous birdlike creature that destroys and devours the Shokopiwah people who attempt to stand against It. While both It's spider and bird forms refer back to earlier iterations and descriptions of Pennywise, these forms both further mark It as uncanny, a recognizable form that is simultaneously alien, in this case because of the monster's literal extraterrestrial nature.

Skarsgård's Pennywise also dons a new and distinctive makeup design. As with other elements of Pennywise's look and performance, there is an unsettling disconnect here between innocence and monstrosity, as Muschietti "envisioned his Pennywise to be something akin to a childlike creature ... [with] bunny teeth, big eyes, and round features."[37] Pennywise has a white-painted face, but rather than that whiteness serving as a clean and even slate, it is weathered and distressed, particularly in the prominent cracks that furrow his high, domed forehead. As with some other elements of his costuming, this brings "a doll-like quality"[38] to Pennywise's look, as though he could be an old and poorly treated porcelain toy. Pennywise's cheeks are prominent and round, lending his face a soft and childlike innocence directly at odds with his intent. The domed forehead, rounded cheeks, and slightly bulbous nose are prosthetic additions to Pennywise's look, transforming Skarsgård's face with a fullness and roundedness that blurs the lines between human and monster, innocence and terror. Pennywise's bulbous head is topped with swoops of orange hair, with voluminous wings sweeping back on either side, though much like the muted palette of the rest of Pennywise's costume, this orange is subdued. The bottom half of Pennywise's nose is painted red, rather than the traditional clown's rubber ball-style nose.

The other signature element of Pennywise's makeup design is his red lips, including lines that go up from the corners of his mouth to continue up his cheeks, then through and over his eyes. When adult Beverly meets It in its Bob Gray persona while trying to escape her childhood apartment, a more organic possibility is presented for Pennywise's distinctive lines, as It taunts her while applying the white makeup that forms the foundation of It's Pennywise face before raising its hands to its own face, gouging the skin there with its nails, and tracing the lines down through its closed eyes, across its cheeks, and in toward the corners of its mouth, with deep cuts and running blood outlining the same pattern as that which appears on Pennywise's painted, finished face. The monster continues to torment Bev with its face half on, an unsettling combination of recognizably human features, half-applied clown face, and intense, watering eyes as It stares down the hallway, physically distanced but emotionally all too close in Bev's recollection of her father's abuse in this same apartment.

Figure 8. Putting on It's Pennywise face

Pennywise's mouth itself is malleable and monstrous by turns. In his exaggerated smile, Skarsgård distends and droops his lower lip, amplifying the curve and profile of Pennywise's smile. In addition to the unsettling mirth of the smile itself, this also showcases the prominent, yellowed top front teeth of Pennywise's usual smile, though this horror is further intensified when its various feeding faces are on display. In one such manifestation, Pennywise has layer upon layer of sharply pointed teeth that emerge from his jaw. The movement of Pennywise's jaws in this incarnation is reminiscent of a great white shark, with the teeth emerging from the rest of the monster's face as it makes the killing bite, as in the attacks on Georgie, Victoria, and Dean. The framing of these attack scenes provide the viewer with a range of perspectives on Pennywise's monstrous mouth and illustrates the different ways in which It terrorizes both victims and enemies alike. In Pennywise's first attack on Georgie in the storm drain, his transformation is filmed in profile, showing the full range of this terrifying change. In his attacks on Eddie in the house on Neibolt Street in *IT Chapter One* and on Victoria under the bleachers in *IT Chapter Two*, the camera is positioned over the victim's shoulder (to the left for Eddie and to the right for Victoria), once again placing the viewer in the subjective position of the victimized child. But when Pennywise unveils his monstrous smile again in preying on Dean in the funhouse, the camera features his face head-on: Pennywise's aim here it to torment Bill (rather than exclusively to terrorize the child before him, as he did with Georgie, Eddie, and Victoria), so the camera aligns the viewer's perspective with Bill rather than with Dean. This horror and the lead up to It's attacks on these children are also compounded by Pennywise's strong propensity to drool, salivating at the fear emanating from his young victims and anticipating the feast to come, with long runners of drool preceding his attacks and dripping all over Eddie in his struggle with Pennywise in the house on Neibolt Street before his friends arrive to rescue him.

Beyond the horror of Pennywise's monstrous layers of sharp teeth, an even greater terror lies within, revealed when Pennywise catches Beverly within It's "deadlights." Rather than feeding on Beverly, It opens its face expansively, with the hinges of these new jaws extending along the painted lines that bisect Pennywise's eyes, revealing a depthless vagina dentata-esque chasm lined with row after row of teeth, with the bright light of It's true essence—It's deadlights—deep within. Pennywise is unable to frighten Beverly but It's deadlights succeed in entrancing her, levitating her in a state of suspended animation and trapped in the limbo of It's power. This expansive release of It's deadlights is central to the adult Losers' final showdown as well, this time with Richie caught by the deadlights and Eddie marshalling his courage to fight, temporarily darkening the deadlights and releasing Richie from their thrall.

Finally, there are Pennywise's eyes. When Pennywise first meets Georgie, his eyes are a bright and vibrant blue, only changing to a deep and reptilian yellow when Georgie leans close and It goes in for the kill, a transformation that is repeated in subsequent attacks. Pennywise's yellow eyes throughout the rest of *IT Chapter One* and *Chapter Two* clearly mark It as monstrous and inhuman, a key feature in marshalling the anxiety of the uncanny, a clear indicator of something not quite right and likely dangerous. Even more unsettling, however, is their unfixed nature, as Pennywise is often looking in two directions at once, with one eye fixed on whoever he is talking to while the other stares blindly off to one side.[39] This sense of unmoored disconnection serves as a warning, but one that often comes too late, as when Georgie's popcorn giggles come to an abrupt halt when Pennywise's eye shifts to one side and the clown's attention slips, leaving him unfocused, still, and drooling. As Georgie and Beverly both discover, however, unfixed does not necessarily mean distracted or safe, as their planned escapes—Georgie in stepping back from the storm drain and Bev in running for the door in the cistern—are stopped, with Pennywise coming immediately back to alertness and violence.

The costuming and makeup design for Pennywise in Muschietti's *IT Chapter One* and *Chapter Two* both draw on traditional clown imagery and depart from contemporary visual representations, including Curry's iconic performance as Pennywise in Wallace's miniseries. The historical influences reflected in Pennywise's costuming highlight the monster's age-old nature, the muted and ephemeral elements allow him to fade in and out of specific locations and scenes while remaining an ever-present threat, and several design details reveal It's extraterrestrial, inhuman nature, evoking images of dolls, spiders, and aliens. Pennywise the Dancing Clown is It's favorite and most frequent form, one that allows for both fun and mayhem, and the elements and significance of this clown figure are central to the design of Muschietti and Skarsgård's Pennywise though, as these unnerving elements serve to remind victims and viewers alike, It is never really just a clown.

WHAT IS IT?

While It takes on myriad forms, externalizing and transforming into its victims' worst fears, none of those reveal It's true self. So with all of It's masks and glamours cast aside, what is It? This uncertainty follows the horror convention of what Martin Rubin calls "the cipher format," in which "the question becomes not so much whodunit but whatdunit,"[40] veering from human violence into monstrosity, which requires a separate framework and set of responses to neutralize the threat. This mystery is never an easy one to solve because, as Jeffrey Jerome Cohen explains, the monster exists in a state of "category crisis,"[41] impossible to compartmentalize or define.

It is an alien presence, a being of near limitless power, the base corporeal form of which is a triad of lights, the deadlights It uses to entrap first Bev and later Richie. Muschietti's conception of It's true form and the Ritual of Chüd that the Losers hope will defeat It is an inversion of traditional Western conceptions of light and darkness, in which light is representative of goodness and knowledge while darkness represents evil, corruption, and danger. This Cartesian duality is problematic and culturally specific rather than a universal perception or "truth." As Theresa H. Pfeifer explains:

> In the Eurocentric ideology of oppositional pairs of categories, the undialectical opposition of white-black, light-dark, good-bad, clean-dirty results in the color *white* being perceived as good and *black* as evil. Black as the symbol of evil and death is not a cultural universal but a peculiar characteristic of Western masculine-biased culture—in many cultures white is the more nefarious color.[42]

While the established Eurocentric duality avers that light will banish darkness, in It's deadlights, the very opposite is true: light is the danger and darkness is the Losers'—and Derry's—only hope of salvation, as they close their eyes and collectively chant to "Turn light into dark" (*IT Chapter Two*). This inversion of the Cartesian duality aligns the Losers and this final showdown with pre-Western cultural beliefs and acknowledges the timeless nature of the monster they face. Established epistemologies and understandings of the world are invalidated, as the power the Losers must draw from to defeat It demands that they suspend their disbelief in order to see and fight It, as everything they have believed to be true of the wider world is called into question. Within the Cartesian duality, "Darkness represents stark absence, a lack, the void of emptiness."[43] In returning to Derry and rediscovering the memories they have repressed, the Losers take ownership of and find power within the darkness, acknowledging and claiming that darkness, marshalling their individual and collective strength as they attempt to contain and extinguish It's deadlights. The Losers have come back to Derry and descended into the dark void of their own lost memories and childhood horrors and, rather than emerging from that darkness into light, they have found meaning, strength, and the solidarity of love and friendship within the darkness itself.

This cosmic reality of It's disembodied nature also presents both narrative and cinematic challenges, raising the question of how—and whether it is even possible—to represent the unrepresentable. When the monster has no form, how can our heroes fight? If it defies intellectual conception and categorization, how can it be contained? If It's true essence has no physical body, what will the viewers see? The Ritual of Chüd presents It in its truest form, as three rapidly cycling orbs of light descending into the cavern beneath the cistern, harnessed and drawn by the Losers' sacrifice of their symbolic tokens. These deadlights also entrap Bev in *IT Chapter One* and briefly snare Richie in *Chapter Two*. However, this true form is also one that the Losers cannot stand against, cannot contain within the Shokopiwah ritual vase as It forces its way out once more, emerging in the form of an enormous red balloon, a symbol of It's clown persona writ large. The crux of the Losers' final showdown with It—and the source of the majority of the horror they suffer in their encounters with It—rely on the creature's ability to change form at will, taking on the appearance of whatever will most terrify its victims, an ability that proves both its great strength and its great weakness, as the monster reverts to a variation of its clown form, in this case with Pennywise's head atop an enormous spider body.

Much like the Shokopiwah ritual that allowed the Losers to entrap and (however temporarily) contain It, it is Shokopiwah wisdom that shows them the way to defeat It, as Mike reminds his friends of the adage that "All living things must abide by the laws of the shape they inhabit" (*IT Chapter Two*). While clowns are figures of the uncanny and have long been a source of uncertainty and terror—and perhaps never more so than in the popular culture moment of Muschietti's films—the clown has also been a figure of ridicule, powerlessness, and abuse, a perspective the Losers draw upon to attack and diminish Pennywise. As Carroll argues, in defusing the potential horror of the monster, it is necessary "to subtract the fearsomeness from this monstrous equation … Once their fearsomeness is factored out, what remains is their status as category errors, which, of course, make them apt targets or objects of incongruity humor."[44] In transferring perceptions of the incongruous from the realm of the uncanny to that of the laughable, the monster is reframed and rendered powerless, stripped of its capacity for horror.

The power of words and speech play a particularly significant role here as well. As Anderson explains in his linguistic analysis of King's work, the name "It" is incredibly powerful, as without any clear meaning or identity, "'It' is merely a referent to the creature that cannot be imagined or described."[45] In this intersection of horror and linguistics, "naming something gives one power over it. Once named, an object can be controlled, a monster destroyed … An entity with no name doesn't fit the formula and is therefore difficult, perhaps impossible to destroy, as it is difficult or impossible to name."[46] As a result, naming and identifying It, harnessing it with a clear and concrete identity, is the essential first step the Losers must take in working to defeat It, and here the figure of the clown and the word itself have power, which can be drawn on and employed not just by It but by the Losers as well. The meaning of the very word "clown" is reclaimed and resituated in this final showdown, harking back to a definition that fits Pennywise very aptly, with its source "in words that mean 'clod,' 'clot,' and 'lump'—i.e. formless masses of stuff, like earth or clay, coagulating or adhering together."[47] This is a particularly fitting definition for the monster here, which cycles through countless forms, malleable and unfixed, as it shifts to take on the appearance of whatever will terrify its victim the most, a process that is rendered effectively impossible by the Losers' rejection and their collective support of one another.

Notes

1. While *Joker* is firmly situated within the larger universe of DC Comics adaptations, it features a wide range of horror genre elements, prompting *Cinema Blend*'s Will Ashton to ask "Wait, Is *Joker* a Horror Movie?" (*Cinema Blend*, 24 Oct. 2019, https://www.cinemablend.com/news/2482941/wait-is-joker-a-horror-movie). Ashton breaks down the arguments both for

and against considering *Joker* as a horror film, ultimately leaving it up to individual viewers to decide how they choose to engage with and interpret the movie.

2. Quoted in Tim Walker, "What is Behind America's Hysterical Obsession with Creepy Clowns?," *Independent*, 6 Oct. 2016, https://www.independent.co.uk/news/world/americas/america-s-hysterical-obsession-creepy-clowns-a7349586.html.

3. Noël Carroll, "Horror and Humor," *The Journal of Aesthetics and Art Criticism*, vol. 57, no. 2 (1999), 146.

4. Carroll, 155.

5. The majority of clowns are male (Benjamin Radford, *Bad Clowns* [Albuquerque: University of New Mexico Press, 2016], 20), so I have used he/him pronouns in describing general clowns and clowning trends here.

6. Carroll, 150.

7. Sigmund Freud, *The Uncanny*, translated by David McLintock (New York: Penguin, 2003 [1919]), 125.

8. Mark Dery, *The Pyrotechnic Insanitarium: American Culture on the Brink* (New York: Grove Press, 1999), 76.

9. Linda Rodriguez McRobbie, "The History and Psychology of Clowns Being Scary," *Smithsonian Magazine*, 31 July 2013, https://www.smithsonianmag.com/arts-culture/the-history-and-psychology-of-clowns-being-scary-20394516/.

10. Quoted in Dery, 72.

11. Dery, 72.

12. Aja Romano, "The Great Clown Panic of 2016 is a Hoax. But the Terrifying Side of Clowns is Real," *Vox*, 12 Oct. 2016, https://www.vox.com/culture/2016/10/12/13122196/clown- panic-hoax-history.

13. Matthew Dessem, "The Wave of Evil Clown Sightings Is Nothing to Worry About. It Happens Every Few Years!," *Slate*, 3 Oct. 2016, https://www.slate.com/culture/2016/10/evil-clowns- have-been-sighted-all-over-america-since-1981.html.

14. Frank T. McAndrew, "The Psychology Behind Why Clowns Creep Us Out," *The Conversation*, 28 Sept. 2016, https://www.theconversation.com/the-psychology-behind-why-clowns-creep-us-out-65936.

15. Quoted in Wax, 157.

16. Michelle Leigh Gompf, "The Disturbing Appeal of Pennywise," *The Many Lives of IT: Essays on the Stephen King Horror Franchise*, edited by Ron Riekki (Jefferson, NC: McFarland, 2020), 114.

17. Gompf, 115.
18. Quoted in Radford, 21.
19. While this painting is only fleetingly and incompletely glimpsed in passing as Bev runs away from from her abusive husband, an image of it—including Pennywise's face emerging from the shadows over Tom's shoulder—is included in Wax (117).
20. Dave Fagundes and Aaron Perzanowski, "The Fascinating Reason Why Clowns Paint Their Faces on Eggs," *BBC*, 6 Dec. 2017, https://www.bbc.com/future/article/20171206-the-fascinating-reason-why-clowns-paint-their-faces-on-eggs.
21. Stephen King, *IT* (New York: Viking, 1986), 13.
22. King, *IT*, 14.
23. Savannah Di Leo, "It: 5 Reasons Why Tim Curry's Pennywise Was Iconic (& 5 Why Bill Skarsgard's Was Nightmare Fuel)," *Screen Rant*, 2 Oct. 2019, https://www.screenrant.com/it-pennywise-tim-curry-bill-skarsgard-comparison/.
24. Marjorie Galas, "For Award Consideration: Costume Designer Janie Bryant's Work in 'It,'" *LA411*, 11 Dec. 2017, https://www.la411.com/blog/post/it-costume-designer-janie-bryant-emmy-winning-costume-design.
25. Dave Trumbore, "'It': Bill Skarsgård's Creepy New Pennywise Costume Revealed," *Collider*, 16 Aug. 2016, https://www.collider.com/it-movie-pennywise-costume-bill-skarsgard/.
26. Quoted in Trumbore.
27. McRobbie.
28. Smith, 184.
29. Trumbore.
30. Trumbore.
31. Galas.
32. Wax, 67.
33. Trumbore.
34. Galas.
35. Galas.
36. Galas.
37. Wax, 166.
38. Trumbore.
39. This is an effect Skargård happened to be able to naturally do on his own, no CGI required. This control is not common for most people with strabismus, a condition in which one's

eyes point in different directions, making this representation of monstrosity potentially problematic.

40. Quoted in Richard Nowell, *Blood Money: A History of the First Teen Slasher Cycle* (London: Bloomsbury, 2010), 22.
41. Jeffrey Jerome Cohen, "Monster Culture (Seven Theses)," *The Monster Theory Reader*, edited by Jeffrey Andrew Weinstock (Minneapolis: University of Minnesota Press, 2020 [1996]), 40.
42. Theresa H. Pfeifer, "Deconstructing Cartesian Dualisms of Western Racialized Systems: A Study in the Colors Black and White," *Journal of Black Studies*, vol. 39, no. 4 (2009), 533, original emphasis.
43. Pfeifer, 534.
44. Carroll, 156.
45. Anderson, 118.
46. Anderson, 118.
47. Carroll, 155.

Chapter 4: Adolescence, Abjection, and Fear

IT Chapter One focuses on the Losers' childhood experiences in Derry, including their conflict with Pennywise, the horrors each encounters in their individual homes, and the collective apathy of Derry in the wake of a rash of missing children. Wallace's miniseries largely bifurcates the Losers' narrative, with the first installment primarily focused on their childhood recollections and the second installment on their adult return, though these two time periods are effectively drawn together by Mike's calls to the adult Losers in the first installment and childhood flashbacks in the second. However, Muschietti further complicates the narrative pattern of *IT* by infusing childhood flashbacks throughout *IT Chapter Two* that do not just add to that earlier story but illuminate and actively reframe it. In doing so, Muschietti positions the first chapter as a film that does not stand on its own, a narrative that is not self-contained, underpinning his vision of *IT Chapter Two* as not a sequel, but a continuation of the same singular and cohesive work. In addition to the narrative complexity of the two films' interaction and engagement, the fears of the Losers' childhoods and Muschietti's representation of them are shaped by nostalgia, the Gothic tradition of externalizing internal horror, sexuality, and collective strength.

IT and 1980s Nostalgia

The nostalgia impulse has been a constant presence in popular culture, with books, television shows, movies, and games inviting the consumer to immerse themselves in an earlier, fondly remembered moment. Keith Naughton and Bill Vlasic note that "social experts say much of the appeal of nostalgia stems from a longing to return to simpler times,"[1] though these "simpler times" are never as ideal and uncomplicated as the rose-colored glasses of nostalgia would suggest. Rather than being inherently better, the notion of the past reflected in the nostalgia impulse instead foregrounds a fictionalization that Stephanie Coontz addresses in her book *The Way We Never Were: American Families and the Nostalgia Trap*, presenting an earlier time, self, and culture that never properly existed.[2] The nostalgia impulse follows a 30-year cycle, reflected in the

1980s' popular cultural boom of television shows and films that invoked and idealized the 1950s, as well as in the 2010s' popular culture obsession with the 1980s reflected in *Stranger Things* (Netflix, 2016–2022) and *IT*,[3] among others. This nostalgia cycle is especially pronounced in the making—and remaking—of *IT*, with King's nostalgia for the 1950s in his 1986 novel, which is echoed in Wallace's miniseries, as well as the 27-year interval between Wallace's miniseries and Muschietti's *IT Chapter One*, a span of time that taps into both the 30-year cycle of nostalgia and the 27-year rest that punctuates It's cyclical return.

Muschietti's Derry is steeped in 1980s iconography, from New Kids on the Block and the *Streetfighter* arcade game to the *Gremlins* (1984) and *Beetlejuice* (1988) movie posters that adorn Bill's walls, which are both films that highlight intersections of humor and horror, an approach Muschietti's own films use to great effect. The titles that grace the theater marquee are also all 1989 releases, including *Batman*, *Lethal Weapon 2*, and *Nightmare on Elm Street 5: The Dream Child*, serving as both a pop culture barometer and a source of nostalgia for viewers. Echoing King's own incorporation of contemporary popular culture references in his work, Muschietti's central engagement with these 1980s elements creates a complex and multilayered setting that invokes nostalgia, alongside the fear that soon encroaches upon this familiarity.

While one straightforward explanation for the reliable recurrence of this nostalgia cycle is the coming-of-age of that earlier generation, who have now become consumers and cultural creators with a desire to buy and recreate their own imagined pasts, this nostalgia impulse also reflects the often complicated ways we think about our individual and collective pasts, construct narratives about ourselves and our histories, and engage with the wider world of the past, present, and future. Not all nostalgia is created equal or stems from the same romanticizing impulse, however. Svetlana Boym distinguishes between two major types of nostalgia: restorative and reflective. As Boym explains this difference: "Restorative nostalgia stresses *nostos* (home) and attempts a transhistorical reconstruction of the lost home. Reflective nostalgia thrives on *algia* (the longing itself) and delays the homecoming—wistfully, ironically, desperately."[4] Lindsay Ellis adds a third type of nostalgia to this framework, that of deconstructive nostalgia, which includes the longing for a previous time but simultaneously critiques that earlier moment, acknowledging its shortcomings, dangers, and fears alongside more idealized nostalgic recollection.[5]

Muschietti's *IT* films engage with all three types of nostalgia outlined above in a complex synthesis, both in the Losers' recalling their own childhoods and memories of Derry and in the viewers' nostalgic engagement with their own individual and collective recollections, whether of King's novel, Wallace's miniseries, or the 1980s. *IT Chapter One* trades largely in reflective nostalgia, emphasizing the children's laughter and camaraderie; while there are plenty of supernatural and domestic horrors, the overall emotion is one of triumphant togetherness, with some of the most traumatic and divisive memories repressed, lacunae that are only revealed and examined in *IT Chapter Two*. The members of the Losers Club literally return home in *IT Chapter Two*, enacting a significant process of restorative nostalgia, though this is similarly complicated by the recollection of their darker and more horrific memories, as well as those of their division and isolation in the splintering of the group following their encounter with It at the house on Neibolt Street. Of these three types, however, Muschietti's *IT* films are most closely aligned with deconstructive nostalgia. Despite the happy memories they have of their shared childhoods and in their reunion with one another, "overall, the film does not paint a very comforting picture of the '80s,"[6] which includes not just the terrors of Pennywise, but the Losers' complicated and, at times, abusive relationships with their parents, the apathy of a community that offers very little protection for its children, and the threat of violence and even death at the hands of Henry Bowers' gang. Each character also recalls the past in markedly different ways, engaging in their own personal experience of nostalgia. For example, while Ben recalls his love for Beverly—reflected in the film through slow-motion, sun-drenched shots that foreground his subjective point of view—when he asks Bev about her memories of their childhood in *IT Chapter Two*, her first instinctive response is "I remember being scared shitless," the emotional tenor of her recollections shaped by terror in contrast to Ben's idealized and wistful longing.

This 1980s nostalgia also engages with King's larger literary and popular culture landscape, particularly in the frequent comparisons critics made between *IT Chapter One* and Rob Reiner's 1986 film *Stand By Me*, an adaptation of King's 1982 novella *The Body*. Both films feature a collective group of kids who are grappling with their own mortality and a world that does not care very much what happens to them. Tasha Robinson furthers this comparison, noting:

> The child protagonists in both *Stand By Me* and *It* are outcasts and nerds, largely ignored and forced to find comfort in each other. They're all hunted by a pack of ferocious, dangerous bullies—bigger kids who are bored with their sleepy town, and victimize other people for entertainment. Both groups of kids set out to look for a corpse, and along the way, they become each other's emotional support, with all the idealized intensity and simplicity Stephen King always puts into evoking childhood.[7]

The nostalgia of *Stand By Me* is one of the 1980s reflecting on the 1950s—the same as the time frame of King's novel and Wallace's miniseries—though the longing for an earlier and more idealized time resonates throughout each version of *IT*. Reviewers also repeatedly drew comparisons between *IT Chapter One* and the Netflix series *Stranger Things*, as both engage in the contemporary 1980s nostalgia boom and build their narratives around the collective strength of a group of kids.[8] In addition to the nostalgia impulse mobilized in Muschietti's films, *Stand By Me*, and *Stranger Things*, each also raises the question that it may not be what these kids survive or when they survive it, but who they survive it with that really matters, prompting nostalgia not just—or even primarily—for an earlier, simpler time, but for the friends with whom they shared it, those emotional connections, and the strength and safety of their collective group.

TERROR, HORROR, AND THE GOTHIC

As Pennywise preys upon the children of Derry, he does so by tapping into their worst fears, by externalizing and mobilizing their internal terror. As Mike hypothesizes in the Losers' first collective conversation about It, "maybe It knows what scares us most and that's what we see" (*IT Chapter One*). This externalization is central to the larger Gothic tradition and particularly to what David Punter identifies as the "'New American Gothic' ... [which deals] in landscapes of the mind, settings which are distorted by the pressure of the principal characters' psychological obsessions."[9] In their encounters with It, what the Losers each see is a physically realized proxy, an externalization of their internal fears, which are impossible to articulate or contain.

This externalization is both empowering and limiting: on the one hand, once a terror can be named, it can be fought, mastered, and brought down to size, as they realize in their adult confrontations with Pennywise, in both Eddie's choking of the leper and in the Losers' collective use of the word "clown" to shrink Pennywise and make it possible for them to destroy It. But, on the other hand, that externalization can only ever be a proxy, a stand in. Their real fears remain unrepresentable, either narratively or visually on the screen. Betty Ripsom's dismembered body, for example, is a gory surprise, but it is ultimately one that Bill and Richie can shut the door on. Derry's apathy to the violence and death that stalk its children cannot be so easily contained or dismissed, however. The realization that the adults are unable (or unwilling) to protect them and the fear that they themselves could go "missing," with no hope of ever being rescued or found, profoundly shapes the Losers' understanding of their town and their precarious position within it, which is a fear that can never be effectively neutralized or defeated. Additionally, the externalized horror can arguably never live up to the imagined horrors in the viewers' own minds, even if the special effects are of the highest quality. This is one of the chief challenges of Muschietti's films, which must mobilize horrors both visible and unrepresentable as each of the Losers comes face-to-face with a symbolic manifestation of their own greatest fears.

As each of them struggles with their own individual terrors, the Losers' fears are rooted in abjection. As Julia Kristeva explains the abject:

> There looms, within abjection, one of those violent, dark revolts of being, directed against a threat that seems to emanate from an exorbitant outside or inside, ejected beyond the scope of the possible, the tolerable, the thinkable. It lies there, quite close, but it cannot be assimilated … A certainty protects it from the shameful—a certainty of which it is proud holds on to it. But simultaneously, just the same, that impetus, that spasm, that leap is drawn toward an elsewhere as tempting as it is condemned. Unflaggingly, like an inescapable boomerang, a vortex of summons and repulsion places the one haunted by it literally beside himself.[10]

When It taps into each of the Losers' fears, those horrors reflect the Losers themselves, in their darkest secrets and the parts of themselves they struggle with, conceal, or reject. In this way, the terrors they must face are multiplied and complex:

the fear of Pennywise himself is the most pressing horror, the one that carries immediate stakes of survival, while the forms It takes to terrorize each of them reflect what they fear the most, a psychological onslaught that threatens to paralyze them in the face of Pennywise's assaults.

These attacks also tap into their more everyday fears, such as parents who are supposed to keep them safe but prove ineffectual or even abusive, and police who are unable to do anything to stop Pennywise's predation on the children of Derry. Timothy Shary explains that "in all forms of horror, youth are endangered not only by their own innocence and ignorance, but also by the authorities that should be protecting and educating them. Time and again, parents, police, and teachers are either feeble or simply prey to the same evil as their young charges,"[11] which allows the violence to continue unchecked. The kids exist largely in a world of their own, with little adult intervention or guidance and, as Andrew Barker notes, "when adults do break into the narrative, they're invariably drunk, cruel, manipulative and indifferent if not hostile toward the fears and worries of those they ought to be protecting."[12]

Finally, what they fear is also internalized, an abjection of the self, so even once the external terror has been survived, the internal abjection remains and, as a result, each individual's sense of self and identity is contentious and fractured, a reality that is returned to and amplified in *IT Chapter Two*. A close consideration of each Loser's respective horrors illustrates these multiple levels of abjection and each character's personal experience and negotiation of fear.

One of the driving horrors throughout *IT Chapter One* is the death of Georgie Denbrough and Bill's inability to come to terms with this loss. Months after Georgie's death, Bill continues to hold onto the hope that his brother is alive, insistently referring to him as "missing" rather than dead and constructing an elaborate series of pipes from his hamster's tunnels to test where Georgie's body should have come out if it had been swept into Derry's sewers. Georgie's body becomes a collective symbol of the Losers facing their own mortality in the body of another murdered child. Bill's obsession with finding Georgie works on multiple levels of abjection as outlined above, as well as drawing on horror's central interconnection of the internal and the external. The first level of abjection here is the body itself, what Kristeva would term "the improper/

unclean."[13] Georgie's body is not Georgie: through its abuse, dismemberment, and death, Georgie's body has become Othered, made monstrous, though Bill still longs to see and hold this body. Denied the opportunity to say goodbye, to navigate his grief and achieve closure through burying his brother, this desire is complicated and, through the influence of Pennywise, corrupted. In Bill's two encounters with the undead Georgie, in his basement and in the cistern, Bill is promised this reunion and closure, particularly in Georgie's plaintive desire for Bill to restore their broken family, as Georgie pleads with Bill to "Take me home, Billy … I miss you. I wanna be with Mom and Dad" (*IT Chapter One*). While Bill is devastated by this encounter, the destruction of Georgie's body and his undeniable death remain visually prominent, as the undead Georgie who reaches out to Bill does so with only one arm.

Bill's desperate hope for this restoration points to another level of abjection and horror mobilized here, as the people who are supposed to keep him safe and protect him have left him largely on his own. Bill is unable to cope with his loss and grief alone, but his parents have proven similarly unable to help him do so. The domestic space has been fragmented and, as Bill tells his friends on the steps of the house on Neibolt Street, "I go home and all I see is that Georgie isn't there … Walking into this house, for me, it's easier than walking into my own" (*IT Chapter One*). Through the loss of Georgie and the isolation he feels from his parents, Bill's home has become a place of hostility and little comfort. He cannot undo what happened to Georgie and he cannot fix the fractures that have separated the remaining members of his family, but he is also unable to accept reality as it stands. As a result, he becomes fixated on taking action: first, in his obsession with finding Georgie and, when he realizes that impossibility, with defeating It, willing to die in the attempt if this proves similarly impossible. Finally, Bill's complicated grief for Georgie is built on a repressed abjection of self, in his overwhelming sense of guilt over Georgie's death, which remains unarticulated and unspoken throughout *IT Chapter One*, a secret and a burden that Bill cannot share with his fellow Losers, even in their closest moments.

Eddie's fears are particularly grounded in abjection's preoccupation with the internal and external, the self and Other. Eddie is desperate for a consistent and reliable way of protecting himself from the dirtiness of the world, a way to stay clean. In a logical and safe world, there is a clear separation between these dichotomies of clean and unclean, an established border or boundary that ensures this compartmentalization and the possibility of cleanliness—or even sterility—that such unequivocal separation offers.[14] Eddie's focus on cleanliness is fanatical, not open to negotiation or compromise. That which is dirty is bad, dangerous, and must be kept separate from the self at all costs, reflected in Eddie's anxiety about the greywater of Derry's sewers and his fanatical directing of the first aid treatment Ben needs after being attacked by Bowers. This filth, however, is inescapable and, in order to cope in a world filled with such unremitting dangers, Eddie has developed a series of coping mechanisms, protections, and talismans to keep himself safe and hold the unclean at bay, with two fanny packs jammed full of his inhaler, pills, and other items that promise to restore cleanliness and order. When Eddie sees It, it is in the form of a leper, a personification of the unclean, what he describes as "a walking infection" (*IT Chapter One*) with bits of the body literally disintegrating and falling off, a worst possible scenario of the unclean run amok. Just as with Bill and his parents, Eddie's fear and trauma has a source within the domestic space as well, in Eddie's domineering mother, who reinforces Eddie's perception of his "delicate" nature, with her control masked behind a justification of protection and love, even as she isolates him from his only friends.

Eddie fears both his perceived weakness and his capacity for strength and bravery, not entirely sure who he is or what he is capable of, and terrified of testing these limits to find out. When Gretta tells Eddie that his medications are placebos, his terror is compounded and turned inward, as he works to figure out why he has been so comfortable existing within the limitations his mother has placed upon him, rarely challenging her definition of him and the control she exercises over his body, his life, and his sense of himself. In this fear of self, these is also a desire for the abject, because in staying limited by his perceived physical ailments and through the buffering protection of his mother—and in *IT Chapter Two*, his wife, who is played by the same actress—Eddie does not have to directly face this fear, which, in some ways, is a fear of himself. Standing up to his mother, telling her that he knows his medications are placebos (or "gazebos" as he calls them), and physically defying her in running out of the house to reunite with his friends and save Bev is a defining moment for Eddie, though his fear of contagion, his perception of his own strength and weakness, and how he sees himself through his mother's eyes are harder to escape. When Eddie joins his friends to reenter the house on Neibolt Street to save Bev, he tosses his fanny pack aside into the overgrown front yard, rejecting his sense of self that has been defined by weakness and sickness, though the inserted scenes of *IT Chapter Two* reveal that he later goes back to reclaim it, with his abjection here mixed with shame, relief, and the comfort of familiarity.

Richie's fear is also deeply rooted in a fear of self and self-knowledge and when he sees It, it takes the form of different versions and proxies of Richie himself, first in a missing poster that he finds in Neibolt Street with his picture on it and later, in the dead Richie doll lying in a coffin in a room full of clowns, after he has been separated from Bill and lured into this dark room when he thinks he sees Eddie and hears his friend calling to him. When the Losers are comparing notes on their greatest fears and the terrifying things they have seen around Derry, Richie's self-professed fear is clowns, though this is a red herring, an inauthentically expressed phobia that masks his real fear of others discovering that he is gay. While much about the 1980s is nostalgically presented in Muschietti's *IT* films and the larger popular culture nostalgia boom, an often marginalized or silenced reality is the emergence of the AIDS epidemic and the hostility toward and abuse of gay men that came along with it, particularly in the early days when fear was high and little about the virus was understood, except for its pronounced impact on gay men. This context would certainly color Richie's experience of his own self-realization, which would be further complicated by growing up in a conservative small town and the rhetoric of homophobic slurs and abuse in the Losers' encounters with Henry Bowers and his gang, including Bowers publicly threatening young Richie and calling him a "faggot" when Henry finds Richie playing video games in the arcade with his cousin (*IT Chapter Two*). While Richie's sexuality is more clearly established in *IT Chapter Two*, in *Chapter One* Richie's interactions with others are often acts of deflection, as he uses humor to keep anyone from getting to know him too well or getting too close, with his biggest fear being his own truth and the rejection and violence to which it could expose him.

As the new kid in Derry, Ben's main desire is to make friends and fit in, though he himself serves as a figure of abjection for many of his peers who, when they are not calling him simply "New Kid," are abusing him with names like "Fat Boy" and "Tits." Difference and exclusion are central to the adolescent hierarchy and Henry Bowers and his friends single Ben out. When Henry Bowers attacks Ben with a knife, the bodily trauma of Henry's attempt to carve his name into Ben's stomach doubles down on the abjection: first, the physical borders between internal and external are violently and painfully breached when Henry cuts Ben and, second, Henry's attempt to override Ben's self-efficacy by carving his own name onto the other boy's body jeopardizes Ben's sense of selfhood and individual agency. Faced with this unbearable abjection, Ben is able to fight back in a way that he has been unable to do before, kicking Bowers to free himself and tumbling down the steep hill that descends into the Barrens, opting for this self-selected trauma, violence, and physical injury rather than that which Bowers attempts to force upon him.

However, while Bill, Richie, and Eddie come to Ben's rescue following Bowers' attack, it is Bev who is able to help restore Ben's sense of selfhood and self-determination, following up her initial concern with an inside joke and a covert wink that helps Ben once more reclaim and reinvest himself with an identity that transcends his trauma and the other boys' responses to this violence. Ben's encounters with It hinge on this fear of isolation and not belonging, first in his pursuit by the headless boy from the Derry Iron Works explosion—a horrific moment in Derry's dark history that he is researching when the librarian Mrs Starret (Elizabeth Saunders) asks him why he has no friends—and later, in a terrifying nightmare in which Bev herself becomes the enemy, berating him and calling him "fat and gross and disgusting" (*IT Chapter Two*) shortly before her head bursts into monstrous flames. Driven in part by his fear of being rejected, Ben works to contribute something valuable to his fellow Losers in sharing his research and knowledge about Derry's history and while this poses the risk of him becoming doubly abject—as a fat kid *and* a nerd—this information proves invaluable to the Losers' survival. Bill, Eddie, and Stan are stunned and unsettled by what Ben has found, though Richie rejects this accomplishment, again deflecting the potential for horror and working to delay the Losers' coming face-to-face with what is really going on in Derry through humor, as he declares there is "nothing cool" about Ben's research (*IT Chapter One*). While Bill's obsession with and questions about the well house on the old Derry map validate Ben's work, it is once again Bev who validates Ben himself, in her discovery of Ben's New Kids on the Block poster on the back of his bedroom door and the secret they keep between themselves.

While Bev validates Ben's identity and selfhood in these key moments, her own is complex and contested. Much like Ben, she is placed in a position of abjection among her peers, in this case because of her reputation as a "dirty girl" (*IT Chapter One*) and her perceived promiscuity. Gretta and her friends dump wet garbage on Bev and call her a "slut" and a "little shit," and Henry Bowers grabs his crotch and tells Losers Club boys that "She'll do you. You just gotta ask nicely … like I did," a degrading and sexualized taunt that spurs the rock war in which the Losers stand against and defeat Henry and his gang (*IT Chapter One*). Word of Bev's rumored promiscuity extends beyond the realm of middle school gossip and bullying, with Derry's adults commenting upon it as well, as Eddie's mother, Mr Keene, and Bev's own father use this perception to exclude and exploit her. Even the boys of the Losers Club briefly discuss Bev's "reputation," though Bill immediately shuts this speculation down, dismissing it as "just rumors," which deflects the conversation into a sweeter consideration of infatuation and romance with Bill and Bev's kiss in the third-grade school play (*IT Chapter One*).

The abjection and abuse Bev faces at home are darker yet. The hair and blood that explode from the sink in her bathroom signify the horror of her own coming of age, maturation, and menstruation, which is made terrifying through her father's sexualization and abuse. As with so many of the Losers Club's real-life horrors, Bev's sexual abuse by her father remains largely unseen and unarticulated, particularly in *IT Chapter One*, when Bev's father smells and intimately strokes her long hair—which prompts her to chop it all off, with this jettisoned femininity becoming part of the horror that emerges from the sink drain—along with his repeated question of "Are you still my girl?" As Bev navigates her transition into young womanhood, she struggles with this abjection both as a result of her "reputation" and her father's abuse. She cuts her hair off in an act of defiance and response to trauma, a rejection of her own burgeoning womanhood, though in doing so—and further abjecting herself in her father's eyes, with revulsion in this case offering potential protection—Bev discovers her own identity and power. As she cuts off her hair, she frantically repeats "This is what you did" (*IT Chapter One*), words that could implicate her father, indicate own abjection and internalized sense of shame, single out and reject the femininity of her long hair, or some combination of these, a complicated and emotionally charged response to her father's abuse.

When It takes on the face of her father in the Losers' final showdown in the cistern and Bev violently rejects and silences him, this is but an echo of her real-life defiance of her father before she was taken by Pennywise, in her resounding rejection of his possessive query and her physical acts of self-defense when he attacks her in an attempt to reclaim his ownership.

The mobilization of Stan's fears are complex, hinging on his sense of who he is and how he understands the world around him. Stan's first encounter with It is through the guise of Judith (Tatum Lee), a painting in his father's office that is brought to terrifying life. Even before heading to his father's office, Stan already has a heightened sense of his difference and inadequacy, as he has just been berated by his rabbi father for being unable to complete the Torah reading for his upcoming bar mitzvah, a failure that underscores both the ways in which Stan falls short of his father's expectations and his own uncertainty about this upcoming rite of passage and its signification of what it means to become a man.

Stan's complicated feelings about these things and his sense of his own filial and religious abjection inform and influence his horrific encounter with the painting of Judith in his father's office. Muschietti notes the similarity of this Judith painting to the style of Amedeo Modigliani, whose "portraits are all women with no eyes. The eyes are empty and he has a tendency to stretch the faces and the necks."[15] The figure of Judith that Stan encounters, both in his father's office and later in the sewers, is distended, monstrous, and grotesque, a clear visual horror. The painting is also an externalization of Stan's more overwhelming fear of chaos and uncertainty. As Wyatt Oleff, who plays young Stan, explains, "He's not only afraid; he's offended" by the distorted proportions and visual wrongness of the painting.[16] This perception is amplified by the tilted angle of the camera as Stan looks at and then straightens the painting, aligning the viewer with the visual perspective of Judith herself as Stan makes this adjustment to its positioning, while simultaneously underscoring Stan's own unease and his rejection of disorder. This horror is further compounded when Judith emerges from her frame and Stan "can't handle her being in his reality because that just doesn't connect."[17] This rejection and inability to accept the impossible impacts Stan's experiences of It and the Losers Club's collective encounters with It as well: when the others are sharing their own experiences, finding comfort in the realization that they are not alone and talking about what they have seen, Stan refuses this understanding of the world, saying "it isn't real. None of this is … None of this makes any sense. They're all like bad dreams" (*IT Chapter One*). When he is forced to come face-to-face with the reality of this horror, attacked by It in the form of Judith in the sewers, he becomes hysterical and when the Losers are called back to Derry as adults, Stan cannot face these horrors, though he also rationalizes his choice to "take himself out of the equation"[18] through his suicide as a means of protecting his friends.

Figure 9. Tilted Stan

Finally, Mike is an ultimate outsider in Derry: he is Black in an overwhelmingly white community, he is home-schooled and thus outside the collective community of his peers, and rumors abound about his parents, as he carries the perceived burden of their legacy. Mike encounters significant racially motivated violence at the hands of Henry Bowers and his gang, who try to run him down in the alley outside of the butcher shop where Mike is delivering meat and, later, when Henry attempts to kill Mike while taunting the other boy with the fire that killed his parents, including Henry's lament that he is "sad that I couldn't have done it myself" (*IT Chapter One*). Mike is separate from the larger Derry community but occupies a space of abjection and not-belonging in his own family as well, as he finds himself unable to live up to his grandfather's expectations of him and rejects the legacy of his parents, saying "I'm not my dad, okay?" (*IT Chapter One*). Mike's parents died in an apartment fire and the commonly held story around Derry is that they were mentally ill drug addicts, responsible for the fire and their own deaths, "bad" people who are not worthy of mourning or grief. When Mike encounters It, it is at the confluence of these two points of abjection, as arms emerge from behind the padlocked butcher shop door, with the sound of flames and cries for help echoing Mike's own childhood trauma in witnessing the fire. The door springs open, revealing the form of Pennywise lurking deep within the meat cooler, though before It can emerge to feed, Bowers and his gang nearly run Mike down, with the supernatural and real-life horrors of Derry colliding in this terrifying moment.

However, while Mike is clearly established—and even self-identified as—an outsider, he is also the one who has the clearest big-picture sense of what is going on and is able to provide his fellow Losers with the knowledge they need to be successful and stand against It. Ben's historical research and Bill's dad's map of the sewer system are valuable pieces of the puzzle, but Mike is the one who has a cohesive explanation, that all of the bad things are really "one thing. An evil thing that feeds off the people of Derry" (*IT Chapter One*) that takes an infinite number of forms. Through his grandfather's stories, Mike has knowledge that the others lack and takes the lead in this defining conversation. Within this scene, Mike's knowledge proves to be paramount and of integral importance, connecting him to his new friends and providing the Losers with insight into Derry's larger history of violence.

As each of these individual encounters demonstrates, when the members of the Losers Club face It on their own, this experience encompasses both the seen and unseen, physical and emotional horrors, the self and the Other. The form It takes for each of them presents a complex negotiation of what terrifies them, both in the wider world and within themselves. These childhood fears are also indicative of the adults each of the Losers will become, providing a glimpse into the people they will be and the things that will still terrify them, the parts of themselves they will ignore, repress, or deny.

Gender, Horror, and the Male Gaze

Representations of gender in horror have been complicated and at times contentious, ranging from images of feminine monstrosity to the survivor strength of the slasher's Final Girl. Horror films have also offered a range of opportunities for navigating narratives of specifically female-gendered traumas, like the rape-revenge films of *Last House on the Left* (1972; remade in 2009) and *I Spit on Your Grave* (1978; remade 2010) and explorations of female sexuality in *Teeth* (2007), *Jennifer's Body* (2009), and *It Follows* (2014).

In her landmark book *Men, Women, and Chainsaws: Gender in the Modern Horror Film*, Carol J. Clover outlines the role and importance of the Final Girl. After the slasher has murdered and mutilated an untold number of victims, the Final Girl is the one left standing: "She alone looks death in the face, but she alone also finds the strength either to stay the killer long enough to be rescued (ending A) or to kill him herself (ending B)."[19] This trope has a rich tradition in the horror genre, including *Texas Chain Saw Massacre*'s (1974) Sally Hardesty, *Halloween*'s (1978) Laurie Strode, and *Scream*'s (1996) Sidney Prescott, to name just a few. While most of these Final Girls start the film as one girl among several, in *IT* Bev is not just the Final Girl, she is the *only* girl.

The only other girls of comparable age to Bev and her fellow Losers featured in *IT* are Gretta and her friends, who ostracize and abuse Beverly, clearly demarcating the lines between Bev and themselves, calling her "trash" and a "slut" in their bathroom altercation on the last day of school (*IT Chapter One*). While Beverly does not have close female friends, she soon finds support and camaraderie with the Losers Club. She is capable of holding her own with the boys and often even surpasses them in ingenuity and bravery, providing a distraction that allows the boys to shoplift the first aid supplies they need to take care of Ben after his fight with Bowers and being the first to jump from the quarry ledge while the boys all stand around in posturing hesitation. She defends herself against bullies like Henry Bowers, kicking off the rock fight with her first throw as she both comes to Mike's defense and violently negates Henry's sexual objectification and harassment of her. She is the only one who does not raise her hand at the house on Neibolt Street when Bill asks his friends who wants to wait outside and she is the first to stand up in the Barrens when Bill asks for their promise to return if the monster comes back. Bev briefly assumes a "damsel in distress"-type role when she is abducted by Pennywise and taken to the cistern in the sewers beneath Derry, from which she has to be rescued by her friends, though even in this abduction she remains brave, defiantly telling Pennywise "I'm not afraid of you" (*IT Chapter One*).[20] Pennywise breathes in Bev's scent to determine whether she is telling the truth, in an unsettling echo of her interaction with her father that draws parallels between these two dangerous figures.

Bev's relationship with her father is abusive and traumatic. In King's novel Bev's mother is present—if ineffectual, like so many other parents in Derry—but, in both Wallace's and Muschietti's films, Bev and her father are alone. King's novel and Wallace's 1990 miniseries depict this relationship as controlling and overbearingly paternalistic, with occasional physical violence and a "barely restrained incestuous urge."[21] However, in Muschietti's films, the tension and palpable threat in Bev's relationship with her father and the abuse that defines it is much more overt, as he frequently touches Bev and repeatedly asks her "Are you still my girl?" (*IT Chapter One*). After a cringingly intimate exchange between the two of them, in which her father smells and strokes her hair, Bev locks herself in the bathroom in a nearly hysterical state of panic and cuts off her hair, relieved when her father is later disgusted by her new appearance, scolding her that it "Makes you look like a boy" (*IT Chapter One*). When Bev's father hears that she has been hanging out with several boys, his first instinctual suspicion is that she has been doing "womanly things" with them, a sexualizing and possessive query as he aggressively caresses her hand and tells her that "I know what's in boys' minds when they look at you, Bevvie. I know all too well" (*IT Chapter One*). Beverly's breaking point comes when her father reaches out to touch her following this exchange, as she evades his grasp and has to physically, violently protect herself from him. He pursues her, knocks her to the ground, and begins to climb on top of her before she is able to escape; she takes refuge in the bathroom, but finally has to knock him unconscious to save herself from his assault.

Of similar horror is her father's unfinished question, when he asks Bev, "Those boys. Do they know that you're my — " (*IT Chapter One*). Cut off by Bev's scream before he can finish the question, the implied completion of his repeated phrase with "girl" carries a range of horrifying ramifications, which Bev cannot bear to hear spoken. *IT Chapter Two* adds further exploration of this relationship, including an exchange between Bev and her father addressing the death of Bev's mother, who committed suicide. After blaming Bev for her mother's death, her father aggressively sprays Bev repeatedly with her mother's perfume and moves to embrace her, saying "You know that I would never hurt you … You know that, don't you?" (*IT Chapter Two*). The tilted camera angle here is used for both subjective and omniscient perspectives, aligning the viewer with Bev's position as her father approaches her with the perfume bottle (though not her literal view, as her eyes are closed) and in a medium shot that uses the tilted angle to underscore her father's physical dominance, the proximity and relationship between their bodies, and the trauma inherent in this relationship and interaction. The look of mingled horror and resignation on Bev's face as she steps into his embrace reveal that this intimacy is not new or even wholly unexpected, but instead something horrifyingly familiar that is to be submitted to and endured.

Just as It remains unnamed throughout the entirety of King's novel and its adaptations, this sexual abuse is similarly "unnamable."[22] As Anderson explains in *The Linguistics of Stephen King: Layered Language and Meaning in the Fiction*, "One cannot effectively name or even articulate what one cannot fully understand or comprehend. If one cannot mean, then one cannot say."[23] With this in mind, Bev's silencing of her father carries tremendous weight: if she stops him from saying it, she can perhaps protect herself from this sexual abuse and the inevitable ramifications of its reality, whether in threat or action. Brown notes than in the 1990 miniseries version of *IT*, the appearance of Pennywise as played by Tim Curry "suggests all kinds of potential horrors, both vicious and sexual, but suggest is all he does,"[24] leaving much of the horror to the viewer's imagination. While this restraint in the 1990s miniseries may have been a workaround of television's Standard and Practices regulations, in many ways the unseen is more horrifying than that which is explicitly shown. While the violence of Pennywise is frequently more overt in Muschietti's films—compare the scenes in which Georgie is killed by Pennywise, for example, with the off-screen violence of Wallace's version contrasted with Georgie's severed arm, gushing blood, and attempted escape in Muschietti's—the sexual abuse Bev endures at the hands of her father remains off-screen, unshown and implied, and all the more horrifying for its peripheral position as it hovers around the edges, most overtly engaged in Bev's father's clear attempt to rape her in this last confrontation and when It takes on the face of her father in the Losers' final showdown in the sewers in *IT Chapter One*.

Laura Mulvey's theory of the male gaze is also a productive tool for reading gender in horror. As Mulvey argues: "In a world ordered by sexual imbalance, pleasure in looking has been split between active/male and passive/female."[25] Within this paradigm, "The determining male gaze projects its fantasy onto the female figure."[26] In horror, this gaze can carry multiple significations, including sexualized objectification and the predatory stalking that is often foregrounded by camera angles that assume the slasher's point of view. The male gaze is complexly negotiated in Muschietti's *IT Chapter One*. Often, the ways Bev is presented fall into traditional patterns of romantic idealizing or objectification, such as in Ben's eyes watching Bev over the top edge of his yearbook as she signs it and the gold-tinted slow-motion shot from Bill's point of view as Bev walks toward him down the street from Keene's Pharmacy.

Figure 10. Bev and the idealizing male gaze

While these shots represent Bev as the idealized feminine and fall into the tradition of Mulvey's male gaze, they also stand in stark contrast to how Bev is seen and viewed by her father and by Mr Keene, whose gazes are exploitative, sexually objectifying, possessive, and demeaning (see Figure 5). Bev's apartment is visually oppressive and darkly shadowed and, within this setting and the scope of her relationship with her father, high-angle shots of Bev abound, putting her in deep shadows and a visually disempowered position as her father looms over her, imposing his will and his body upon her. In her interaction with Mr Keene at the pharmacy that enables the boys to steal the first aid supplies they need to help Ben, Bev takes advantage of the ways in which she can control and manipulate the male gaze, drawing Mr Keene's attention, flattering him, and even talking him into letting her try on his glasses, a physical echo of the ways in which she is co-opting and manipulating his gaze. While Bev remains in control of her interaction with Mr Keene and even swipes a pack of cigarettes for her trouble while his back is turned, that does not make his gaze any less predatory or objectifying, and Bill's idealizing gaze as Bev walks down the street toward him serves as a visual corrective, a way of looking that is not demeaning or dangerous.

Another key moment in which the male gaze is significant is after the Losers go swimming in the quarry, when the camera assumes the position of the boys' gazes and emphasizes their overt fascination with Bev's half-clad body as she lays in the sun in her bra, underpants, and big sunglasses while Young M.C.'s "Bust a Move" plays in the background. Even though these particular shots also fall into the pattern of what Mulvey refers to as "*to-be-looked-at-ness*,"[27] these images and this narrative moment are empowering, rather than objectifying, exploitative, or dangerous, like the gaze assumed by her father or Mr Keene. Instead these are moments in which Bev is seen and valued, and, even more importantly, moments in which she exercises overt agency, deciding who sees her and how they see her, as well as establishing clear control of her own body. In many ways, Bev has to fight for this control of and agency over her body, as her peers project the rumors of her "reputation" onto how they see and treat her, while at home she is unable to protect herself from her father's physical and sexual abuse. In the space and experiences she shares with her fellow Losers, she does not have to worry about her physical safety or the abuse of her body: she can let her guard down around them, she can embrace and explore her own relationship with her body and her sense of self outside the realms of the multiple abuses to which it is otherwise subjected, and she can touch, lean against, and embrace her friends without any fear that this intimacy could veer into exploitation or violation. The easy physical connection she has with her friends and the kiss she shares with Bill at the end of *IT Chapter One* are moments of choice, agency, and action, as Bev works to define a relationship with her body that is not dictated by the transgressed boundaries or abjection of assault and abuse, all of which subvert and surpass the "*to-be-looked-at-ness*"[28] of the exploitative gaze.

Collective Power

Each member of the Losers Club is confronted by their deepest fears and must bear their own individual trauma. However, it is the combined power of the Losers Club that is the key to their defeat of Pennywise. Each of the Losers escapes Pennywise's predations when they encounter It alone, either by running away or having those attacks interrupted. Getting away is important, of course—it saves their lives—but this escape only forestalls the inevitable, with the Losers knowing they could encounter It in any of its forms around any corner in Derry. Individually, they are surviving, but they are not winning. In order to stand against Pennywise, to fight back, and to hurt It, they have to do so together, drawing on their collective power and the bonds of camaraderie, trust, and friendship that unite them, following a contemporary pattern in which "Youth in most horror films have evolved beyond the survival of violence to the conquering of fear."[29] The Losers are separated as they enter the house on Neibolt Street, with Bev, Ben, Mike, and Stan waiting outside while Bill, Richie, and Eddie go in; once inside, Bill, Richie, and Eddie are similarly isolated from one another. However, when they save Eddie and fight Pennywise in the kitchen, it is as a unified and collective group. They are attacked and injured, but they survive and gain knowledge about Pennywise that they did not have before, learning the secret to tracking and hopefully defeating It. As Bev reminds her fellow Losers in the aftermath of this confrontation: "We were all together when we hurt it. That's why we're still alive" (*IT Chapter One*). This is not enough to pull the group back together, however, and when they are separated from one another It grows in power and influence, which enables It to take Bev.

While *IT Chapter One* offers a brief montage that bridges the gap between the Losers' separation and reunion, *IT Chapter Two* delves more deeply into those days of separation, with each adult member of the Losers Club traversing Derry in search of their token while simultaneously recovering the repressed memories of the childhood days they spent apart. When they are separated as children, It preys on each of them again but, this time, with no one to turn to for support or solidarity, the Losers internalize this trauma, retreating into silence. Bill devolves further into his own self-hatred in blaming himself for his brother's death. Richie endures Henry Bowers' humiliating attack at the arcade and internalizes this rejection and shame. Bev stands up to and is violently attacked by her father, while Eddie becomes once more complacent under the smothering attentions of his mother. Ben retreats to his previously friendless and bullied state. Mike assumes the mantle his grandfather has passed him, finally able to kill the sheep, and he remains silent when he overhears people whispering about his parents at the butcher shop. Stan's further childhood horrors remain largely untold, as he is not there to recall or recount them, though the Losers' collective memories of young Stan foreground his fear of disconnection and the self-doubt he expresses in his bar mitzvah speech. Their separation and isolation from one another leave them each vulnerable physically, psychologically, and emotionally. Their lives are endangered and their well-being is compromised, as they lose both their safety and their sense of who they are in the absence of their friends' love and acceptance.

The Losers are brought back together when Pennywise takes Bev and while they are again separated and preyed upon as they make this rescue effort—in Bowers' attack on Mike in the house on Neibolt Street, Judith's assault on Stan, and Bill's pursuit of and final confrontation with the undead Georgie—they are soon reunited, with the Losers rallying around Mike, rescuing Stan and Bev, and embracing Bill in the aftermath of these individual horrors. When Pennywise attacks them in the cistern, the Losers fight for one another: Bev strikes against Pennywise to save Bill, while Mike is quick to attack when Pennywise turns to threaten Bev.

Pennywise makes one final attempt to separate the Losers from one another, offering to let the rest of them go free if they leave Bill with him, making the bargain that "I will take him, only him … and you will all live to grow and thrive and lead happy lives" (*IT Chapter One*). There is a moment of dramatic tension as the members of the Losers Club seem to consider this possibility and the seemingly insurmountable odds of standing against Pennywise. Bev is once again the force that initially works to hold the Losers Club together, just as she was when they found Bowers and his gang attacking Mike, in expressing solidarity with Bill on the steps of Neibolt Street, and in the aftermath of their first confrontation with Pennywise. But in this case it is Richie who has the final word. He builds suspense and dramatic tension in a subversive deployment of his usual wisecracks, working to lull Pennywise into a sense of complacency as he says: "I told you, Bill. I fucking told you. I don't want to die. It's your fault. You punched me in the face. You made me walk through shitty water. You brought me to a fucking crackhead house, and now … I'm gonna have to kill this fucking clown" (*IT Chapter One*). Brought back together, against overwhelming odds and even when they have been offered a way out, the Losers actively choose to stand together and with one another. This solidarity throws Pennywise off-balance, as It cycles through multiple forms and faces, unable to zero in on a single, salient terror that will be the most effective, given the Losers' diverse range of fears and their collaborative assault.

While each is faced with familiar horrors—along with some new ones, including the mummy that attacks Ben and the giant spider arms that foreshadow one of It's final forms in *IT Chapter Two*—in this showdown, the Losers do not have to face these fears alone and their friends are there to fight with them, defend them, and save them. In the final confrontation, the Losers stand together to save one another from their own worst fears as It cycles through a litany of horrors: Stan saves Mike when It uses burned and grasping arms to attack Mike, Bill rescues Ben from the mummy, and Ben saves Mike from the partially transformed spider creature. However, bolstered by the support of their friends, the individual Losers also strike back at their own worst fears, with Stan beating Judith and Eddie kicking the leper. Bev sees her father and, in an echo of their fight in the apartment, silences him before he can finish his repeated and unsettlingly intimate question, this time silencing the word "girl" with the phallic penetration of a piece of rebar jammed down his throat, an even more violent negation than that which she voiced in the apartment above, before backing away in stunned horror. While each of these combative responses—whether in fighting for themselves or for one another—are essential to the Losers' defeat of Pennywise, they are only truly effective when they all act together, attacking Pennywise in tandem and advancing upon him as he backs away from them, injured and afraid.

As they stand together in the Barrens following their fight with Pennywise, the collective strength and solidarity of the Losers Club is of central importance, even as they prepare to go their separate ways. Their pledge to one another, with their cut palms and their clasped hands, signify that this separation is different from the one following Neibolt Street, and while the ties between them may be stretched thin and even temporarily forgotten, that strength and solidarity will not be compromised, there for them to rediscover when they are called back again 27 years later.

Notes

1. Keith Naughton and Bill Vlasic, "The Nostalgia Boom," *Business Week*, no. 3570 (1998), 60.
2. Stephanie Coontz, *The Way We Never Were: American Families and the Nostalgia Trap* (New York: Basic Books, 1992), 9.
3. Patrick Metzger's 2017 analysis "The Nostalgia Pendulum: A Rolling 30-Year Cycle of Pop Culture Trends," *The Patterning*, 13 Feb. 2017, https://www.thepatterning.com/2017/02/13/the-nostalgia-pendulum-a-rolling-30-year-cycle-of-pop-culture-trends/ provides data on filmmaking remake trends, including the number of years between original films and their remakes or reboots, as well as a detailed list of nostalgically remade or rebooted films from the late 1990s through the late 2010s.
4. Svetlana Boym, "Nostalgia and Its Discontents," *The Hedgehog Review*, vol. 9, no. 2 (2007), 13.
5. Lindsay Ellis, "Stranger Things, IT and the Upside Down of Nostalgia," *YouTube*, 4 Dec. 2017, https://www.youtube.com/watch?v=Radg-Kn0jLs&feature=youtu.be.
6. Ellis.
7. Tasha Robinson, "Stephen King's It is the Rare Monster Movie with Too Much Monster," *The Verge*, 6 Sept. 2017, https://www.theverge.com/2017/9/6/16257788/it-movie-review-stephen-king-andy-muschietti-pennywise-the-clown.
8. Finn Wolfhard, who played *IT*'s Richie Tozier, is also a central cast member on *Stranger Things* as Mike Wheeler, with his performances in both serving as a frequent point of connection and comparison in these critical analyses.
9. David Punter, *The Literature of Terror: A History of Gothic Fictions from 1765 to the Present Day, Vol. 1: The Gothic Tradition*, 2nd ed. (Oxfordshire: Routledge, 1996), 2.
10. Julia Kristeva, *Powers of Horror: An Essay on Abjection*, translated by Leon S. Roudiez (New York: Columbia University Press, 1980), 1.
11. Timothy Shary, *Generation Multiplex: The Image of Youth in American Cinema after 1980* (Austin: University of Texas Press, 2014), 173.

12. Andrew Barker, "Film Review: Stephen King's 'It,'" *Variety*, 5 Sept. 2017, https://www.variety.com/2017/film/reviews/it-review-stephen-king-1202547601/.

13. Kristeva, 2.

14. Kristeva, 4.

15. Quoted in Wax, 15.

16. Quoted in Wax, 144.

17. Oleff quoted in Wax, 144.

18. Wax, 145.

19. Carol J. Clover, *Men, Women, and Chain Saws: Gender in the Modern Horror Film* (Princeton: Princeton University Press, 1992), 23. Clover first presented her analysis of the Final Girl in her 1987 article "Her Body, Himself: Gender in the Slasher Film," which became the first chapter of *Men, Women, and Chainsaws*.

20. This damsel-in-distress moment follows familiar fairy-tale trajectories, which is particularly significant within the well-established intersections between fairy tales and horror that have been explored by Maria Tatar, Jack Zipes, Walter Rankin, and others. When her fellow Losers find Bev in the cistern, she is caught in It's deadlights, held in a state of supernatural somnambulism or suspended animation. While they are able to pull her down from where she hangs in the air, they are unable to wake her up, until Ben kisses her in the tradition of fairy-tales like those of "Snow White" and "Sleeping Beauty." While the lack of consent is as problematic here as it is in those established tales (a fact acknowledged by his fellow Losers' discomfort), Ben's kiss is successful in awakening Bev, who realizes in this moment that Ben is the one who wrote her the anonymous poem, a connection which is revelatory though fleeting.

21. Tony Magistrale, *Stephen King: The Second Decade, Danse Macabre to The Dark Half* (Twayne's United States Authors Series) (New York: Twayne, 1992), 106.

22. Anderson, 116.

23. Anderson, 118.

24. Brown, 158.

25. Laura Mulvey, "Visual Pleasure and Narrative Cinema," *Feminist Film Theory: A Reader*, edited by Sue Thornham (New York: New York University Press, 1999 [1975]), 62.

26. Mulvey, 62.

27. Mulvey, 63, original emphasis.

28. Mulvey, 63, original emphasis.

29. Shary 167.

Chapter 5: The Return of the Repressed

IT Chapter Two returns to the lives of the Losers 27 years after the horrifying summer of IT Chapter One, exploring the adults they have become and drawing them back home and back to their childhood selves. Muschietti's approach to bridging this gap is complex and interconnected. First, the opening scenes of IT Chapter Two return viewers to the denouement of the first film, including the image of Bev suspended in It's deadlights in the cistern, and Bev's narration of that experience and her vision to her friends, in her premonition of their eventual return. However, even in this opening repetition, Muschietti makes it clear that the first film has not provided viewers with the whole story. Both IT Chapter One and IT Chapter Two include the scene of the Losers in the Barrens, promising to come back if the monster ever returns, but the second film adds elements of dialogue and foreshadowing that were missing from the first film's closing scene, such as Stan asking Bev about what he is like as an adult, to which she replies "Like now, but … taller" (IT Chapter Two), with her tone and facial expression conveying affection and concealed grief in her knowledge of future tragedy. While this repetition and revision of scenes between the two films work to orient viewers as they shift from one narrative to the other, however, it is Muschietti's synthesis of the two time periods and significant expansion of the first film through the lens of the second that is the most notable.

Figure 11. The Losers in the Barrens

IT Chapter One cannot be understood as a self-contained narrative. A traditional sequel adds to the original work, continuing the story as it moves chronologically forward. However, with *IT Chapter Two*, Muschietti moves simultaneously forward and backward in time, synthesizing the two periods and the experiences of the characters. The flashback scenes of *IT Chapter Two* provide additional information about the Losers' childhood summer together, giving both the viewers and the characters themselves further insight and the expanded perspective of adults, as the Losers uncover memories they had forgotten. Through this new awareness, the Losers find themselves reassessing who they were, what they remember, and who they have become, as they navigate both old and new nightmares together.

THE RETURN OF THE REPRESSED

The adult Losers rediscover themselves and their childhood memories in stages. When Mike first calls each of them to come back to Derry, he is nearly a stranger, an unfamiliar name from a faraway place and a long-forgotten past. The sense of familiarity soon returns and while the Losers' memories take a bit longer to come back, their terror is immediate. Their hearts pound and their hands shake; Richie throws up and Eddie crashes his car. Each of the Losers is taken out of their immediate surroundings as where they are and who they have become fall away, amplifying the similarities between their child and adult selves, such as Richie's jokes, Eddie's fixation on risk analysis, and Bev's abusive relationship with her husband Tom.

Stan is the exception to this gradual remembering, responding to Mike's call with near-immediate recognition and asking "It's come back, hasn't it?" (*IT Chapter Two*). While the others are drawn back on the basis of a promise and some as-yet-unremembered camaraderie, Stan remembers everything and his suicide closes the gap between the two time periods, with Muschietti editing together scenes of adult Stan undressing and climbing into the bathtub with his childhood recollections of Bill's face in the Barrens as he asks for Stan's promise. Bill cuts Stan's palm, the slicing of his palm shown in close up rather than the medium shots of the final scenes of *IT Chapter One*, with this reframed narrative recollection paralleling Stan cutting his wrists, which remains unshown, one injury standing in for the other as the lines between past and present deteriorate.

When the Losers are first reunited in Derry at Jade of the Orient, their coming back together is celebratory, filled with energy and laughter as they rediscover one another and fall back into old patterns of connection and inside jokes. There is a funhouse quality to this particular scene, with the Losers' overlapping voices and their bodies in constant motion as they jostle and embrace one another. Even the room itself seems to be in motion: streams of bubbles and swimming fish move through the aquariums that line the walls and a turntable at the center of the table spins in a shot framed from above, with the Losers grabbing food as it zips past. The editing mimics this frenetic engagement with rapid cuts between multiple perspectives: while the camera position remains omniscient, showcasing the Losers as a cohesive whole rather than aligning with any individual character's perspective, the images shuffle quickly between different pairings and groupings, visually emphasizing the multiple connections and conversations that are all happening simultaneously, in cooperation with the overlapping voices, laughter, and music. The dynamics between characters are visually reestablished as well, like Richie and Eddie's energetic joking and the familiar framing of Bill and Bev engaged in conversation as Ben looks longingly on. There are few awkward silences between the Losers and the first memories that return to them and the initial recognition they have of one another is an emotionally charged joy that at times nearly borders on hysteria, with their excitement at rediscovering one another clamoring to drown out the other, darker memories and associations that threaten to surface.

Figure 12. The reunited Losers

However, it is a fundamental truth of the genre that horror will not be denied. Robin Wood notes that "Basic repression is universal, necessary, and inescapable,"[1] essential to self-actualization and a productive navigation of the world. However, repression is fundamentally unsustainable and "what is repressed must always strive to return."[2] As Valdine Clemens explains, the

> "Return of the repressed," or emergence of whatever has been previously rejected by consciousness, is a fundamental dynamism of Gothic narratives. Something—some entity, knowledge, emotion, or feeling—which has been submerged or held at bay because it threatens the established order of things, develops a cumulative energy that demands its release and forces it to the realm of visibility where it must be acknowledged.[3]

The reunion of the Losers Club quickly devolves from revelry to terror, first with the group's collective pause when Ben asks "Is Stanley coming or what?" (*IT Chapter Two*) as the camera pans around to position itself behind the empty chair intended for Stan. This seemingly innocuous disruption and the overt recognition of Stan's absence opens the door to further horror as the Losers share their responses to Mike's phone call and their recollected—though not yet fully remembered—fear. Once this tipping point is reached, their horrors quickly multiply, both physically and emotionally, with the eruption of the monstrous fortune cookies coupled with the enigmatic fortunes within, which, when puzzled together, taunt the Losers with Stanley's absence. Their terror, loss, and sense of collective experience are further complicated with Bev's revelation that she knows how Stan died and has had premonitions of each of their respective deaths. These realizations and the Losers' encounter with the horror that animates Derry nearly rupture their newly reformed connections, with the group dispersing in multiple directions, ready to run.

While the Losers are quickly drawn back together, reinvested in their commitment to one another and the promise they made 27 years ago, this initial separation signals a shift in the nostalgia framework of their reunion. The Losers' coming together at Jade of the Orient engages with Boym's notion of restorative nostalgia: they remember the good things, they find joy and humor in rediscovering one another, and the memories that begin to surface are largely positive ones, with the Losers' camaraderie eclipsing the horrors they endured, at least at this stage in their remembering. Much the same could be said of *IT Chapter One*, in which the emotional tone and narrative focus remain fixed on the kids' friendship and collective strength. There is both horror and trauma, but they overcome it together. They are splintered from one another following the confrontation with It at the house on Neibolt Street, but much of the ugliness of that rupturing is elided with a montage that bridges the gap between their separation and their reunion.

IT Chapter Two is a meditation on memory, the process of remembering, the memories themselves, and the construction of the self and relationship between past and present that such remembering entails. The central role of memory is foregrounded in Mike's voiceover early in *IT Chapter Two*, as he reflects "Memory … it's a funny thing. People want to believe they are what they choose to remember. The good stuff. The moments. The places. The people we all hold on to." While *IT Chapter One* emphasizes the Losers' togetherness and collective strength, this second film requires them to come to terms with the darker parts of themselves, both as children and as adults, a recognition of the reality that, as Mike intones in the opening voiceover of *IT Chapter Two* that closes the gap between past and present, "sometimes we are what we wish we could forget."

However, as Muschietti follows the adult Losers' going their separate ways in the aftermath of this homecoming meal, the nostalgia mode shifts from restorative to deconstructive,[4] with the Losers forced to remember and reckon with their own weaknesses and failures as children, as well as the flawed and fallible nature of their adult selves, a dual consideration that is mirrored in the film's structure as it blurs the lines between these time periods with smooth edits between flashbacks and the present. These transitions are visually negotiated through the physical spaces featured in the film itself, with such shifts occurring when the camera's view enters a storm drain, when Bev descends the ladder into their subterranean clubhouse, or through the closing door of the synagogue where Stan had his bar mitzvah, for example. Muschietti's approach to editing these transitions is complex and achieves multiple aims, blurring the lines between past and present, while simultaneously providing a narrative and visual framework that foregrounds the act of remembering and allows the characters to process and reflect on these remembered moments.

One particularly illustrative and multilayered example of this complex negotiation of visual and narrative transitions between past and present is the Losers' return to their clubhouse. The adult Losers find their old clubhouse, with Ben falling through the hatch and into the space below. As he calls for his friends to come down, the scene seamlessly transitions from the present to the past, with the camera showing the same ladder as young Bev descends, shifting from adult rediscovery to childhood memory. The scene transitions back to the adult Losers as the camera follows the loose ball of Ben's broken paddleball, with adult Eddie reaching into the slats of the pallet under which it rolled to retrieve the ball. The scene transitions back to the childhood Losers, this time connected through Bill reaching into a coffee can to pull out a shower cap, with Bill in the present and a transitional shot looking over Bill's left shoulder segueing to young Richie's point of view of Stan in the past. Finally, the scene shifts back to the present and the adult Losers with Bev telling Stan "You don't have to be so … sad" (*IT Chapter Two*), with the final word bridging the gap between time periods, shifting from the voice of Sophia Lillis to that of Jessica Chastain, a recentering that allows the Losers to collectively reminisce, share their memories of Stan, and acknowledge the significance of both his friendship and his absence. Muschietti also uses these visual transitions to effectively navigate between past and present selves as the Losers consider their childhood memories and the fundamental truth of their identities, such as when adult Eddie walks into Keene's Pharmacy and, in approaching the counter, slips back into his childhood self, with Eddie's eyes serving as the visual point of transition between these two time periods. The final scene of the surviving Losers includes a similar transition, as Bill, Ben, Richie, Mike, and Bev stop to look into a plate glass window in Derry's downtown, which reflects their childhood selves as they are rejoined by Stan and Eddie, with this reflection transitioning back to the young Losers heading home after their confrontation with It.

Overall, the flashback scenes that fill in the gaps in the Losers' individual and collective childhood experiences complicate the narrative and viewer understanding of *IT Chapter One*. While the previously established narrative was one of cohesive togetherness and mutual support, when the Losers are separated from one another, they encounter traumas that, in many cases, they cannot effectively face or process alone. Richie is unable to defend himself against Bowers and his gang in their confrontation at the arcade, without his friends to back him up, or reassure him in the aftermath, and his shame is even more deeply felt because of his own internalized homophobia and his inability to embrace or express who he is, a silence that follows him into his adult life. Bev must face her father's abuse alone, as he berates her and sprays her with her mother's perfume before pulling her into an intimate embrace, without the strength of her friends and the fearlessness she feels when she is with them to counterbalance her powerlessness at the hands of her father. In some cases, the horrors the Losers encounter operate with a kind of dream logic, though even within this skewed perception, the terrors they face reflect their greatest fears, such as Eddie finding his mother held captive and attacked by a leper in the basement of Keene's Pharmacy or Ben's conversation with Bev, in which she rejects and attacks him, her head bursting into flames as she pursues him through the dark, deserted halls of the school. In each of these cases, the Losers' friendship and the reassurance that they can turn to and rely upon one another has been stripped away and each must shoulder this burden on his or her own. This fragmentation also works to call into question the narrative and relationships already established, for while the story of *IT Chapter One* is one of friends who could tell each other anything and count on one another no matter what, as these flashback scenes reveal, they have all been carrying their own secrets and each have parts of themselves that they have kept hidden from the others and that Muschietti has concealed from the viewer. With *IT Chapter Two*'s return to the past, the viewer comes to know these characters in a fundamentally different way, with the idealization of nostalgia stripped away to reveal characters who are more complex, conflicted, and flawed, adding another, deeper layer to the narrative of *IT Chapter One*.

This complicated understanding of Losers' childhood selves is also foregrounded in their final confrontation with It, when the Losers are separated, with many of them sent back to once again face some of their worst childhood traumas and fears. Bev finds herself trapped in a bathroom stall, surrounded by explicit graffiti, while those who have abused or exploited her attempt to beat the door in, including Gretta, Mr Keene, Henry Bowers, and her father. Ben finds himself plunged into the Losers' clubhouse, with a place of fun, safety, and his own ingenuity and potential now threatening to become his grave as the clubhouse fills with dirt; Pennywise's taunts similarly take Ben back to the isolation and fears of his childhood, as he tells Ben that he is "still just a little fat, fat, fatty loser ... who always knew he would die alone" (*IT Chapter Two*). In this case, Bev and Ben are able to rescue one another, to combine their strength and save themselves. When Bev's father once again asks "Are you still my little girl, Bevvie?," this time Bev responds with a resounding and full-throated "Not anymore!" (*IT Chapter Two*), fighting back against the image of her father, the ways in which her life has been shaped by her reputation and others' perceptions of her, and her belief in her own self-worth, which has to this point been compromised in the abusive relationship with her husband Tom that echoes that which she had with her father. In this violent negation, she frees herself not just from the nightmare bathroom stall, but also from the psychological and emotional horrors that have defined her life, relationships, and sense of self. This negation also breaks Bev out of a pattern of passive response that has separated her from the fearlessness of her childhood self, as throughout *IT Chapter Two* Bev is often screaming in horror or shocked into stillness, with a single tear running down her cheek. Ben also must make a choice and give voice to a previously unspoken truth, in this case the poem he wrote to Bev as a boy and his declaration of love for her. Bev is drowning in blood and Ben is being buried alive but, through facing these fears that have silenced them since their childhoods, they are able to break free, save one another, and put themselves once more in a position where they can fight alongside their friends.

Bill is similarly drawn back to an image of his greatest childhood horror, though he must face this one on his own, finding himself in his family's flooded basement, facing an undead Georgie, his own childhood self, and his overwhelming feeling of guilt for his brother's death. While this guilt and sense of responsibility have shaped Bill and informed his understanding of himself since the day he lost Georgie, in this bifurcation of Bill from this childhood version of himself, he is able to objectively see his own pain, find empathy for that younger self, and finally forgive himself. The young version of Bill that adult Bill encounters in the flooded basement verbalizes every horrible thought Bill has had about himself and his role in Georgie's death, including that "We deserve to die ... We killed our little brother" (*IT Chapter Two*). While this is one of It's tricks, intended to plunge Bill into self-loathing and despair by preying upon his own intense feelings of guilt, Bill instead rejects this self-hatred, symbolically murdering his childhood self and at last laying Georgie to rest. Just as Bev needs to deny the narrative of abuse that has worked to define her and Ben must find a way through the silence of his adolescence, Bill has to jettison that part of his childhood self, rejecting the guilt and responsibility that has colored his memories of his youth, himself, and Georgie.

This catharsis is incompletely achieved, however, and, in some cases, the secrecy continues or characters' stories remain undeveloped. Eddie fights past his fear, faltering both in the house on Neibolt Street and in the cistern before finding the courage to launch the fence spike into It's open mouth, only to die as a result. Mike's family history, the discourse of racism that informs both the town's speculation and the narrative construction of his parents' deaths, the relationship he has with that legacy, and how he will move on from a life that has been driven by obsessively focused vigilance are never substantively explored or resolved. Richie's sexuality also remains unaddressed: he never comes out to his friends or tells Eddie how he feels about him. His grief at Eddie's death is devastating and his friends rally around him as they bathe themselves in the quarry, but when Richie goes back to the bridge to reinscribe his and Eddie's initials, he does so alone.[5]

Finally, the critical perspective afforded by deconstructive nostalgia also extends to the Losers' consideration of their adult selves. As they discover in returning to Derry, they are not necessarily who they thought they were when they were children and, as they recognize those flaws, they have to reconsider themselves—and one another—within that newly established framework and shifted perspective. This is most evident with Eddie and Mike. Eddie's view of the world is structured by fear of contagion and the rituals that keep that danger at bay. When he learns as a child that his medicine is a placebo and that the medications are his mother's way of maintaining control over him, he is able to break free of her limiting influence and help his friends, to be a hero alongside them. With his fellow Losers, he discovers the bravery of which he is capable, his stronger and better self. However, what Eddie is forced to contend with as an adult is that, despite this collective strength, his fear still has the potential to paralyze him, even when that paralysis puts his life and the lives of those he loves in danger. When Richie is attacked by the monstrous Stan-head spider in the house on Neibolt Street, Eddie is unable to move, frozen in horror as Bill screams for Eddie to help and the snapping jaws descend toward Richie's face. While Eddie recommits himself to bravery in the aftermath of this attack, when Bev is pulled below the water in the cistern, he stands by, immobilized by fear once again, while the others dive in to rescue her. Eddie needs the strength of his friends, with Bev's makeshift lance that "kills monsters" and Richie's reassurance that "You're braver than you think" (*IT Chapter Two*) to keep moving forward, to face the final horror. In the end, Eddie's fears are actually validated as he makes his heroic contribution to fight against It, saving Richie and making what he believes to be the killing blow. Eddie is a tragic hero who engages in an epic struggle to overcome his fear and his own limitations, only to discover that those fears were well-justified when It strikes with a fatal counterattack. Though Eddie dies, he does so confident in his bravery and his contributions to the collective struggle, not just in having physically stood against It but also in helping remind his friends of the wisdom that gives them the knowledge they need to defeat It.

Mike is a tragic hero of a different sort, with the fatal flaw of hubris. He occupies a privileged position in his knowledge of It: he is the one who stayed in Derry, watches and waits, remembers everything. He has the power to call the rest of the Losers back, to draw them together, to make them remember. He is consumed by this responsibility and obsessed with his research. As the self-appointed expert, he is confident that he knows what must be done and is willing to go to any lengths to achieve it, which leads him to break the sacred bond of trust that is the bedrock of the Losers' collective friendship. When he calls the Losers to bring them back, he does not tell them everything, in this case a lie of omission and even a potentially understandable one: they do not remember what happened in Derry, are not ready to remember when Mike calls them, and are actually much better prepared and supported in this remembering when they are back together. However, the Losers still feel misled and tricked when they discover Mike's subterfuge, with Richie quipping that the "first words out of your mouth should have been like 'Hey man. You want to come to Derry and get murdered?' 'Cause then I would have said no" (*IT Chapter Two*). As the Losers scatter and prepare to flee, Mike makes another conscious choice to deceive Bill. Mike drugs Bill as he tells him the story of the Shokopiwah, confident that if Bill can only see what Mike himself sees, Bill will understand and stand with him. Again, this is a deception that pays off, in which Mike is validated in believing that the end justifies the means. However, there is still a lie residing at the heart of this truth, as Mike conceals the fourth side of the ritual vase and the fate of the Shokopiwah people from Bill and the rest of the Losers, a truth that is only revealed in the midst of their final showdown with It, through which Mike has endangered all of their lives and their very chance of success by not being truthful with them.[6] When Mike defies It, the monster calls Mike "a madman" (*IT Chapter Two*) and this assessment has some merit.[7] He has been consumed by his obsession and, in its pursuit, he is willing to sacrifice everything and everyone, including his best friends.

However, despite these flaws and the deconstructive nostalgia that brings them to light and reframes how these characters see one another, the Losers' dedication to and support of each other remain steadfast. Though they each could have died because of Eddie's inaction, Richie and Bev rally around him to support and encourage him, to empower him and make sure he knows that he is loved and valued. Similarly, though Mike lies to his friends several times over the course of *IT Chapter Two*, his fellow Losers do not abandon or reject him. While deeply flawed, the information Mike has provided them to defeat It is ultimately successful, which seems to cancel out the deceptions that have framed their larger journey. For both Mike and Eddie, their friends' love is unconditional and they do not have to "earn" it back, prostrate themselves, or atone. They messed up, they were not their best selves, and they have been forgiven.

Within the context of this deconstructive nostalgia and their own rediscovery of themselves—both individually and collectively—it is essential that each of the Losers face that self-destructive or limiting perception of themselves and the trauma they had long ago buried. This is why the process of naming It to rob the monster of its power is so integral to their success in their final showdown with It as adults. In the last confrontation of *IT Chapter One*, the Losers face their respective fears as It visually cycles through their nightmares, but in *IT Chapter Two* they instead seize control of the monster's cycling by identifying It's weakness and limitations, calling it an "imposter" and a "mimic" (*IT Chapter Two*), denying it of its power to terrify by reducing it to its performative nature and, finally, shrinking It to manageable size by seeing It as nothing more than a clown. Instead of having to master their childhood fears, when they face It again as adults in this final showdown they have to jettison those same fears, refuse the lies and deceptions of It's terror, and free themselves from the past.

THE SHOKOPIWAH AND THE RITUAL OF CHÜD

One of the most problematic elements of *IT Chapter Two* is the invention of the Shokipiwah and the reimagined Ritual of Chüd. In King's novel, the ritual is a metaphysical battle of the wills, an internalized trial that sends Bill's consciousness out to the very rim of the cosmos to gain understanding of where It has come from and what It is capable of. However, this intensely psychological and internal exploration does not lend itself well to compelling visual representation or narrative filmmaking. Muschietti's reimagining of It's origins and the ritual that can defeat It instead draw from an invented Native American belief system and font of knowledge.

In *IT Chapter Two*, Mike shares his experiences with Bill, drugging his friend so that he can experience the same vision that Mike himself had seen, of the cosmic arrival of It and its pervasive, destructive presence in Derry over the last few million years. Muschietti presents the vision with blurry, distorted visuals of the ceremony itself, the forms It takes to appear to the Shokopiwah, and Mike's own vision, with his body echoing and layered over that of one of the Shokopiwah people as he reaches out, co-opting their experience and perspective. While Mike imposes a narrative explanation onto this vision, the images themselves are fragmented, isolated moments of mysticism and violence, both in Mike's recollection of his interactions with the Shokopiwah and in the dark vision of the form it took to attack them. These blurred images of Mike's vision are intercut with Bill's own terrified response as he cowers in fear, framing this knowledge and the way in which it has been transmitted as violent and traumatic. While this insight is presented as horrifying, it does provide Mike and his fellow Losers with the information they need to defeat It. But both the narrative itself and the way in which Mike assimilates and uses this knowledge is problematic.

First of all, as Jordynn Paz explains, "The Shokopiwah do not, nor have they ever, existed."[8] The Native American culture presented in *IT Chapter Two* is an amalgamation of generic Native American tropes and stereotypes, ranging from the "noble savage" to the "wise medicine man." The Shokopiwah act as a plot device rather than characters or even a community in their own right. Nick Martin notes that "there's no actual attempt to be inclusive or authentically representative … there's not a single line of dialogue for the hazy, drugged-up Natives. Instead, they are simply there, floating around the frame while Mike narrates his trip, more inanimate objects than real human beings with beliefs that demand respect."[9] Their sole purpose is to pass the necessary information on to Mike and then conveniently and silently disappear from the narrative, with no outcry about Mike's appropriation of their knowledge or his theft of the ceremonial vase depicting the ritual. As Paz explains:

> The mystical and magical elements the writers and directors employed in the film are demeaning to [Native American] ceremonies and traditions. Dumbing our sacred practices down to hallucinations and "rituals," reinforces damaging stereotypes that many people in mainstream society believe to be true about our people ... Not only were the fictitious Shokopiwah exploited and stolen from in the movie, they were also killed and pushed to the outskirts of society ... [where] they were conveniently placed when the main characters needed them.[10]

In his telling of this story, Mike frames his encounters with the Shokopiwah as those of a man deferentially seeking wisdom and knowledge, immersing himself in their culture and teachings, though his engagement is actually one of exploitation and cultural appropriation.

When Mike is shown a vision of It destroying the Shokopiwah people who tried to contain it with the Ritual of Chüd, he rejects and erases this experience from his own narrative. The knowledge Mike has gained from the Shokopiwah is essential in identifying It's true nature and figuring out how to defeat It, but in Mike's appropriation of this knowledge, it is instead presented as flawed and in need of "improvement" in order to be truly effective. The Shokopiwah's traditions and knowledge are also depicted as an embodied and traumatizing experience, as visually presented in both Mike and Bill's hallucinations and their horrified responses, in their widened eyes, their screams, and Bill's bloodied mouth. This discourse of trauma stands in direct contrast to the Losers' own storytelling, as they share what they have seen with one another in the town square in *IT Chapter One* in a narrative—rather than intensely experiential—collaboration. Every part of Mike's interaction with the Shokopiwah, from his sense of being entitled to their history and knowledge to the destructive ways in which he appropriates these experiences, is exploitative, and when he has gotten what he came for, he leaves and the Shokopiwah disappear from the narrative, silenced and made invisible, elided once more by the needs of "civilization."

Mike similarly reframes Derry's larger cultural engagement with the Shokopiwah, saying that the Shokopiwah people moved outside of Derry to get "beyond It's reach" (*IT Chapter Two*) rather than acknowledging that they were excluded, driven out, or forced to the margins, a lack of awareness that is particularly striking in light of his own experiences in Derry as a Black man and the discrimination he has faced as a result of his racial difference. While Mike's own subjective descriptions of these interactions almost invariably portray him as positively as possible, when Bill asks Mike how he got the ritual vase, Mike actively negotiates his account of the story before telling the truth: "I found it ... No, no, they ... they gave it to me ... I stole it" (*IT Chapter Two*). While Bill is disapproving in the face of this confession, Mike's explanation quickly moves along with a dismissive "It's complicated," eliding any opportunity for addressing the larger colonial tradition of theft and exploitation of which Mike's actions are a part. Paz's point about Native American knowledge and tools being "conveniently placed" within reach of the heroes in their moment of need is further echoed by the tomahawk on display in the Derry Library, briefly glimpsed by Bill and visually foregrounded by Muschietti before Mike shares his vision with Bill. Later in the film it is close at hand when Bowers attacks Mike, with Richie grabbing the tomahawk and burying it in the back of Bowers' head, co-opting the power of this weapon with no understanding or contextualization of where it has come from, why it is there, or what it means within the larger cultural landscape of Derry, the Shokopiwah, or the exploitative relationship between the two.

Compounding his problematic appropriation of the Shokopiwah knowledge and ritual vase is Mike's belief that his own understanding and use of it are not just equal, but superior to their own. He knows that the Shokopiwah's attempt at the ritual ended tragically, and he defaces the fourth side of the vase to conceal this fact from Bill and the other Losers, desecrating a priceless cultural artifact that he has no right to possess in the first place. When the Ritual of Chüd fails and Mike's deception is discovered, he tells his friends that the Shokopiwah "didn't believe ... They didn't believe they could kill it! That's why it didn't work" (*IT Chapter Two*). Mike has appropriated and violently overwritten the Shokopiwah's account of the ritual by stealing and defacing the vase and, in his criticism of their failure, he is claiming superior knowledge, understanding, and belief, erasing the contributions of the Shokopiwah, identifying them as intellectually and morally inferior, and reenacting the colonial tradition of taking what belongs to Native Americans to put it to "better" use.

In the end, the contributions of the Shokopiwah are even further marginalized and erased in the final confrontation between the Losers and It. While the repeated wisdom that "All living things must abide by the laws of the shape they inhabit" (*IT Chapter Two*) is integral in It being contained, made small, and destroyed, the more specific elements of the Shokopiwah's teaching and ritual are discarded altogether, with the Losers taking this main idea, appropriating and reconceiving it, and putting it to use in their own way, largely divorced from the wisdom and traditions of the Shokopiwah.

Humor, Horror, and Perspective

Several critics found fault with Muschietti's use of humor in *IT Chapter Two*, with James Grebey arguing that the film "is really more of a comedy than it is a horror movie."[11] Horror and humor are interconnected in a range of complex ways, from humor as a release valve in the midst of the horrific to the horror-comedy subgenre that intentionally blends characteristics of both traditions. As Carroll explains: "The basic idea behind the incongruity theory of humor is that an essential ingredient of comic amusement is the juxtaposition of incongruous or contrasting objects, events, categories, maxims, properties, and so on."[12] In other words, humor is derived from the fact that what is being seen does not belong: it is out of place, out of context, out of the logical order of reality or reasonable expectation. This pattern of transgression is central to both humor and horror, with both genres pushing the boundaries, extending beyond the demarcated barrier of what is expected or accepted. In the shocking transgression of boundaries and the body, for example, Stan's decapitated head growing legs and turning into a monstrous spider can simultaneously evoke both horror and humor, particularly given the creature's alternating cycle between laughter and screaming.

There is a significant amount of humor in *IT Chapter One* as well, with insults, one-liners, and inside jokes ricocheting back and forth between the Losers, a pattern immediately reestablished with the Losers' reunion at Jade of the Orient in *IT Chapter*

Two. The balance of horror and humor in *IT Chapter Two* skews more toward the comedic than *Chapter One*, a shift that can be at least partially attributed to the significant change in perspective and different approaches to dealing with horror by the Losers in the second film. The lives of children are full of small everyday terrors, from the boogeyman to the playground bully. Children are also well accustomed to having little control over their own lives, which are largely dictated by their parents, teachers, and other authority figures who determine their daily routines, chores, meals, and bedtimes. With this default of uncertainty and limited power, the young Losers are resilient, negotiating quickly between humor and horror, absorbing the terrifying knowledge of It's long history in Derry, and suffering assaults both human and supernatural, but still maintaining their sense of childlike belief and squeezing in some summer fun, like trips to the arcade and swimming in the quarry.[13] Not only is this horror almost seamlessly integrated into their lives, but their relationships with one another are also heartfelt and earnest, despite the secrets they each keep, as they turn to one another to collectively shoulder the fears they cannot bear alone. As a result, the balance of horror and humor are mutually supportive, with collective humor serving as protection and solidarity to counter the terrors they face. They feel this horror completely and the danger is life-threatening but, in laughing with one another, they are able to recover, recharge, and heal.

Adults are less well-equipped to deal with the inexplicable or respond to disruptions in the logical order of the world, as evidenced by the adults in Derry who look the other way, refusing to see the terrors of their small town. As a result, the humor the adult Losers use is different, often mobilized as a negation rather than an expression of cohesion. As Anna Green notes, one explanation for someone laughing when frightened is that "fearful laughter actually represents a denial of fear. We're scared, but we're trying to convince ourselves and the people around us that we're not—that everything is okay."[14] While the young Losers were able to incorporate these horrors into their understanding of the world and respond to them with collective strength, the adult Losers are unable to do so, struggling to reconcile their childhood memories and their current experiences in Derry with a fundamental understanding of how the world is supposed to work. Viewed through this lens, the Losers' revelry at Jade of the Orient is still joy at rediscovering one another, but it is also a show of bravado, a performance of normalcy to cancel out the terrors they will have to remember and face all too soon, that are waiting just below the level of consciousness, felt though not yet reclaimed.

While the young Losers had no choice but to recognize and respond to the dangers they faced, in order to survive the adult Losers must come at this fear indirectly, through refusal, memory, and humor. Alex Lickerman argues that this use of humor when faced with the horrific is healthy and restorative, saying that "being able to laugh at a trauma at the moment it occurs, or soon after, signals both to ourselves and others that we believe in our ability to endure it."[15] Following this line of reasoning, for the Losers, both as children and as adults, humor is both an integral source of connection and a survival strategy. When the Losers are confronted with the dead body of young Stan—a traumatic return in and of itself—and the monstrous transformation of his decapitated head into a spider-creature, Richie's instinctual, stunned response is "You gotta be fucking kidding" (*IT Chapter Two*).[16] Richie is often the comic relief of the group, just as he had been as a kid. The adult Losers' return to their old clubhouse highlights the occasional dissonance of Richie's humor and the role of his comic interjections, when his friends are horrified by his Pennywise impersonation from the shadows, followed up by Richie's pronouncement that he is "Just trying to add some levity to this shit" (*IT Chapter Two*). His fellow Losers are not amused and, while Richie does not push it, he also does not quit cracking jokes moving forward. In addition to Richie's comic relief, the relationship and exchanges between Richie and Eddie are a significant source of camaraderie and humor, from their childhood argument over the clubhouse hammock to their adult arm wrestling at Jade of the Orient and the countless quips and insults bandied between them as both children and adults that fuel their collective friendship and entertain their fellow Losers. Without these strategies at their disposal, the adult Losers could easily have become paralyzed by their fear, overwhelmed by the horror and unable to sustain the suspension of disbelief that was so easily achieved and empowering as children.

The Ritual of Chüd is an example of this individual and collective use of humor to understand and respond to horror, as well as to connect with themselves and one another. In preparing for the ritual, each of the Losers has to find a token to sacrifice, something representative of their childhood in Derry. Finding these tokens takes them back to those memories and their childhood selves, filling in the gaps and elisions of

IT Chapter One. This token-finding process is challenging and traumatic for many of them, with Richie returning to the scene of Bower's bullying, Bill to the storm drain where Georgie was killed, and Bev to her old apartment and the memories of her father's abuse. However, when the Losers are reunited for the Ritual of Chüd—which really should be serious, suspenseful, and potentially horrifying—humor still makes its way in, particularly in Richie and Eddie's back-and-forth about what will and will not burn. Though these sacrifices are also punctuated by earnestness (Bill's paper boat) and intimate connection (Ben's yearbook page, Bev's postcard), the humor and engagement between Richie and Eddie inject some levity to the process as they work to productively respond to the horrors they are facing and fall back into their childhood patterns and rapport. Laughter—as it so often is for the reunited Losers—is the only way to absorb and survive the horrors they face, to bring them back to themselves and one another, to reclaim the power of their younger selves.

This group dynamic highlights the ways in which the Losers have come back to their childhood selves, reoccupied their previously established roles, and once again embraced the relationships that defined them both individually and collectively, while simultaneously accepting the ways they have each changed as they have grown into adults. Just like their shared horror and the easy camaraderie they fall back into upon their reunion, the Losers' use of humor remains a powerful way of connecting with one another, though the significance and mobilization of this humor has changed, just as the Losers themselves have. This combination of humor and horror echoes the Losers' collective strength, providing them with multiple strategies for rediscovering themselves and their relationships, as well as for standing against and finally defeating It.

NOTES

1. Robin Wood, "An Introduction to the American Horror Film," *The Monster Theory Reader*, edited by Jeffrey Andrew Weinstock (Minneapolis: University of Minnesota Press, 2020 [1979]), 109.

2. Wood, 118.

3. Valdine Clemens, *The Return of the Repressed: Gothic Horror from The Castle of Otranto to Alien* (Albany: State University of New York Press, 1999), 3-4.

4. Restorative nostalgia still plays a significant role in the Losers interactions in *IT Chapter Two*, specifically in how they remember and talk about their lost friends. For example, while reminiscing in the clubhouse, the Losers emotionally reflect on Stan's loss, saying he was "the best" and when they swim in the quarry after emerging from the sewers, they mourn Eddie with their recollection that "He'd be looking out for us. The way he always was." In these two cases, the restorative nostalgia runs counter to earlier constructs and experiences—including Richie's identification of Stan as "the weakest" of the Losers and Eddie's inability to help his friends when he is paralyzed by fear—though it actively reinscribes and folds Stan and Eddie back into the idealized, communal identity of the Losers Club.

5. In considering LGBTQIA+ representation in horror, this is a significant difference from Wallace's miniseries, in which Eddie is the gay-coded character, with "his death indicat[ing] a return to normative gender roles" (June Pulliam, "'Best Not to Look Back': Monstrosity, Medium and Genre in Tommy Lee Wallace's *It* (1990)," *The Many Lives of IT: Essays on the Stephen King Horror Franchise*, edited by Ron Riekki [Jefferson, NC: McFarland, 2020], p. 86). While Richie's survival in *IT Chapter Two* defies the "bury your gays" trope that often sees LGBTQIA+ characters killed in literature, film, and popular culture, he remains mired in a space of repression and silence.

6. Richie catches a brief glimpse of the marred fourth side of the vase in the library before Mike snatches it away from him, with Richie's curiosity a distinct contrast to the ways in which Mike manages and manipulates Bill's perception of the vase and its account of the ritual. In denying Richie's curious gaze, Mike is able to sustain the partial narrative a while longer.

7. This directly echoes Stan calling Bill "insane" when they were children following their encounter with It at the house on Neibolt Street, with Bill and Mike united by their single-minded focus on destroying the monster in the past and the present.

8. Jordynn Paz, "The Real Monster Wasn't the Clown, It was the Cultural Ignorance," *Montana Kaimin*, 27 Sept. 2019, https://www.montanakaimin.com/opinion/the-real-monster-wasnt-the-clown-it-was-the-cultural-ignorance/article_6cde5860-e170-11e9-9b7d-0707847a9f6c.html (this source cannot be accessed in the EEA or the UK).

9. Nick Martin, "Native Spirituality is Not For Sale," *The New Republic*, 16 Sept. 2019, https://www.newrepublic.com/article/155010/it-chapter-two-great-american-tradition-selling-native-spirituality.

10. Paz.

11. James Grebey, "IT Chapter Two Twists Comic Relief into Something Awful," *SyFy Wire*,

6 Sept. 2019, https://www.syfy.com/syfywire/it-chapter-two-twists-comic-relief-into-something-awful.

12. Carroll, 153.

13. In *IT Chapter One*, this summer fun often demarcates the difference between Bill's serious and committed focus on finding It and avenging his brother's death and his friends' denial, resistance, and yearning for the simple pleasures of a childhood summer. As Stan reminds his friends when Bill and Richie venture into the sewer culvert, "It's summer. We're supposed to be having fun. This isn't fun. This is scary and disgusting" (*IT Chapter One*). While Bill enjoys the fun he has with his friends, the conflict with It unwaveringly remains his top priority and he is willing to go to the house on Neibolt Street with or without his friends, following his exasperated exclamation "If you say it's summer one more fucking time …" (*IT Chapter One*).

14. Anna Green, "Why Do We Laugh When We're Scared?," *Mental Floss*, 16 Oct. 2015, https://www.mentalfloss.com/article/69830/why-do-we-laugh-when-were-scared.

15. Quoted in Green.

16. This line is also an echo of and direct homage to John Carpenter's *The Thing* (1982).

Conclusion

Muschietti's *IT Chapter One* and *Chapter Two* are complex negotiations of King's novel and the established popular culture memory of Wallace's 1990 miniseries. But, even more significantly, these films take this familiar narrative in a new direction, with Muschietti's inventive synthesis of the past and present (particularly in *IT Chapter Two*), the addition of new developments and directions for established characters, and a reimagined version of Pennywise the Dancing Clown that has already become instantly recognizable and iconic in its own right.

The story at the heart of *IT* is one of friendship: the ease and camaraderie of adolescent friendship, the nostalgic way in which those relationships are remembered, and the rare but magical rediscovery of those connections as adults. Muschietti perfectly captures this dynamic, including the contradictions and complexities that challenge any easy reading of who these characters are and what their relationships mean. The young Losers' friendship in *IT Chapter One* is largely idealized, one of laughter and—for the most part—the steadfast solidarity of friends who are there for one another, no matter what. King is well-known for presenting realistic and empathetic representations of children and adolescents, from Danny Torrance in *The Shining* (1977) to the paranormally gifted children of *The Institute* (2019), and with *IT Chapter One* and *Chapter Two* Muschietti carries that tradition forward. Muschietti and the young actors have all commented upon the genuine affection and chemistry between the actors who played the Losers in *IT Chapter One*[1] and this rapport carries through to the actors who play the adult Losers in *IT Chapter Two*, with careful casting and established camaraderie between the actors who played the child and adult versions of each character. There is a unique continuity and authenticity of connection between *IT Chapter One* and *Chapter Two*, which is firmly grounded in the intimately interconnected nature of the two films, as the synthesis of the two films' narratives resulted in the actors working directly together, collaborating and building upon their counterpart's own version of the character. In a distinct echo of the power of childhood and imagination central to *IT*, the adult actors came to *IT Chapter Two* with a focus on performing their characters as invented and brought to life by the young actors who came before them; James Ransone, for example, said that in playing adult Eddie Kaspbrak, he focused on "do[ing] the best Jack Dylan Grazer impression I could."[2] As part of achieving this synthesis, each of the young Losers wrote a letter in character to their older selves, reintroducing them to the world of Derry, their childhood selves, and what they need to remember and hold on to in order to survive.[3] This approach to casting, characterization, and connection across the two films is integral in bringing the Losers to life, as children and as adults, as individual characters and as a collective group.

Beyond the characterization and his own take on King's narrative, Muschietti's meditation of memory (again, particularly in *IT Chapter Two*) is masterful. As the Losers—and the viewers alongside them—discover, what one remembers may not be all that there is. Through his implementation of deconstructive nostalgia, Muschietti is able to return to the Losers' childhood selves to simultaneously highlight their truth and their silence, what is remembered and what is repressed. The central position of memory and remembering in *IT Chapter Two* frames the Losers' homecoming as an act of dynamic negotiation, a return to Derry, their past, and themselves, embracing both the nostalgia and the horror as fundamentally inextricable from one another. What we remember, what we forget and why, the idealized memories that overwrite a complicated past, how those earlier memories resurface, and the way we understand ourselves, our experiences, and the world around us as a result are all central to the structure and narrative of *IT Chapter Two*, as well as its engagement and synthesis with *IT Chapter One*. This remembering is both traumatic and affirming: through recovering what has been repressed, the Losers must contend with the darkest parts of themselves, but, in doing so, they gain a more intimate, authentic, and empowering sense of themselves, their pasts, and their friendships.

Through the complication of the earlier narrative, *IT Chapter Two* is messy and disruptive, it challenges what had been a fairly straightforward and familiar buddy film, with these narrative expectations noted in the frequent comparisons of *IT Chapter One* to other works like *Stand By Me* and *Stranger Things*. In *IT Chapter Two*, Muschietti presents an entirely new perspective, dismantling the familiar narrative and requiring viewers to realize that the story we think we know is not the whole story. Silenced voices and hidden secrets hover around the margins, absences that remained invisible until Muschietti filled them in in *IT Chapter Two*, only then inviting viewers to see that those lacunae had been there all along. The untold stories that emerge to fill these voids are often painful—such as Bill's guilt, further details of Bev's abuse, and Richie's terrified silence—and insist that the Losers reexamine who they were, what they experienced, and who they have grown up to become. However, what they find is that they are strong in their survival, enriched by remembering and embracing the parts of themselves they have repressed, and can trust in the love and support of their friends, despite the decades and forgetting that separate them from that childhood summer. The complete story of the summer of 1989 revealed in *IT Chapter Two* is messier, more complicated, and more painful than that of *IT Chapter One* for characters and viewers alike. But its truth, its heart, and the connections that bind the Losers as both children and adults are a satisfying payoff, culminating in the combination of voices that read the final lines of Stan's letter aloud, offering a heartfelt and philosophical reflection on the bond the Losers share.

Through its central focus on remembering, as well as the narrative and visual synthesis of the two time periods in *IT Chapter Two*, Muschietti's film defies the expectation of a traditional sequel, instead providing viewers with two parts of a single, cohesive story, neither of which can be fully understood without the other. In this way, artistic form echoes narrative function, demanding that the viewer themselves consider their own perspective and understanding, requiring them to consider what they might not know, what stories have remained untold, and what secrets have been kept. Even following the Losers' defeat of Pennywise at the end of *IT Chapter Two*, there is a sense that the story might not yet be completely told, with a rumored director's cut or supercut potentially adding even more to the narrative established by Muschietti's two films.[4] There has even been talk of a continuation of Pennywise's story, one that would look backward over It's long and violent life rather than serving as a traditional sequel. While these projects may or may not come to fruition, these speculations affirm the realization that just as *IT Chapter Two* provided a new perspective on *IT Chapter One*, so much of the story remains untold, hidden in the silences and ellipses of the films and *IT*'s larger narrative.

Notes

1. The chemistry and friendships between the young actors are discussed at length in the special features that accompany both films, specifically "The Losers Club" featurette on *IT Chapter One* and the two documentaries on "The Summers of IT" on *IT Chapter Two*.
2. "The Summer of IT—Chapter Two: IT Ends."
3. "The Summer of IT—Chapter Two: IT Ends."
4. Michael Kennedy, "IT: Everything We Know about the Director's Cut & Supercut," *Screen Rant*, 13 Dec. 2020, https://www.screenrant.com/it-movies-stephen-king-directors-cut-supercut-explained/.

Bibliography

Anderson, James Arthur. *The Linguistics of Stephen King: Layered Language and Meaning in the Fiction*. Jefferson, NC: McFarland & Company, 2017.

Ashton, Will. "Wait, Is *Joker* a Horror Movie?" *Cinema Blend*. 24 Oct. 2019. https://www.cinemablend.com/news/2482941/wait-is-joker-a-horror-movie.

Barker, Andrew. "Film Review: Stephen King's 'It.'" *Variety*. 5 Sept. 2017. https://www.variety.com/2017/film/reviews/it-review-stephen-king-1202547601/.

Biodrowski, Steve. "Festival & Funhouse Review: The IT Experience Chapter Two." *Hollywood Gothique*. 23 Aug. 2019. http://www.new.hollywoodgothique.com/it-experience-two-review/.

———. "Haunted House Review: The IT Experience." *Hollywood Gothique*. 9 Sept. 2017. http://www.new.hollywoodgothique.com/haunted-house-review-the-it-experience/.

Boym, Svetlana. "Nostalgia and Its Discontents." *The Hedgehog Review*, vol. 9, no. 2 (2007): 7–18.

Bradley, Laura. "This Was the Decade Horror Got 'Elevated.'" *Vanity Fair*. 17 Dec. 2019. https://www.vanityfair.com/hollywood/2019/12/rise-of-elevated-horror-decade-2010s.

Brown, Simon. *Screening Stephen King: Adaptation and the Horror Genre in Film and Television*. Austin: University of Texas Press, 2018.

Burnham, Emily. "The 1984 Murder of Charlie Howard in Bangor Will Be Dramatized in the 'IT' Sequel." *Bangor Daily News*. 4 Sept. 2019. https://www.bangordailynews.com/2019/09/04/news/bangor/the-1984-murder-of-charlie-howard-in-bangor-will-be-dramatized-in-the-it-sequel/.

Cahir, Linda Costanzo. *Literature into Film: Theory and Practical Approaches*. Jefferson, NC: McFarland & Company, 2006.

Cain, Rob. "2017 Is the Biggest Year for Horror in Decades." *Forbes*. 16 Oct. 2017. https://www.forbes.com/sites/robcain/2017/10/16/2017-is-the-biggest-year-for-horror-in-decades/?sh=5f2ebcb652d9.

Carroll, Noël. "Horror and Humor." *The Journal of Aesthetics and Art Criticism*, vol. 57, no. 2 (1999): 145–160.

Child, Ben. "It's Coming, as Hollywood Plans Stephen King Adaptation." *The Guardian*. 13 Mar. 2009. https://www.theguardian.com/film/2009/mar/13/stephen-king-it-film-adaptation.

Clemens, Valdine. *The Return of the Repressed: Gothic Horror from* The Castle of Otranto *to* Alien. Albany: State University of New York Press, 1999.

Clover, Carol J. *Men, Women, and Chain Saws: Gender in the Modern Horror Film*. Princeton: Princeton University Press, 1992.

Cohen, Jeffrey Jerome. "Monster Culture (Seven Theses)." *The Monster Theory Reader*, edited by Jeffrey Andrew Weinstock. Minneapolis: University of Minnesota Press, 2020 (1996), pp. 37–56.

Coontz, Stephanie. *The Way We Never Were: American Families and the Nostalgia Trap*. New York: Basic Books, 1992.

Crow, David. "It Chapter Two: Adrian Mellon and Derry Hate Crimes." *Den of Geek*. 19 July 2019. https://www.denofgeek.com/movies/it-chapter-two-adrian-mellon-derry-hate-crimes/.

Dery, Mark. *The Pyrotechnic Insanitarium: American Culture on the Brink*. New York: Grove Press, 1999.

Dessem, Matthew. "The Wave of Evil Clown Sightings Is Nothing to Worry About. It Happens Every Few Years!" *Slate*. 3 Oct. 2016. https://www.slate.com/culture/2016/10/evil-clowns-have-been-sighted-all-over-america-since-1981.html.

Di Leo, Savannah. "It: 5 Reasons Why Tim Curry's Pennywise Was Iconic (& 5 Why Bill Skargard's Was Nightmare Fuel)." *Screen Rant*. 2 Oct. 2019. https://www.screenrant.com/it-pennywise-tim-curry-bill-skarsgard-comparison/.

Eco, Umberto. "Innovation and Repetition: Between Modern and Post-Modern Aesthetics." *Daedalus*, vol. 114, no. 4 (1985): 161–184.

Ellis, Lindsay. "Stranger Things, IT and the Upside Down of Nostalgia." *YouTube*. 4 Dec. 2017. https://www.youtube.com/watch?v=Radg-Kn0jLs&feature=youtu.be.

Fagundes, Dave and Aaron Perzanowski. "The Fascinating Reason Why Clowns Paint Their Faces on Eggs." *BBC*. 6 Dec. 2017. https://www.bbc.com/future/article/20171206-the-fascinating-reason-why-clowns-paint-their-faces-on-eggs.

Fischer, Russ. "Cary Fukunaga Explains the Demise of His Unconventional 'IT' Adaptation." *Slash Film*. 3 Sept. 2015. https://www.slashfilm.com/cary-fukunaga-it/#more-312794.

Foutch, Haleigh. "How 2017 Became a Landmark Year for Horror Movies." *Collider*. 21 Dec. 2017. https://www.collider.com/horror-movies-2017-box-office-records/.

Freud, Sigmund. *The Uncanny*, translated by David McLintock. Penguin, 2003 (1919).

Fuster, Jeremy. "'It' Has Broken a Box Office Record Every Day for the Past Week." *The Wrap*. 15 Sept. 2017. https://www.thewrap.com/it-box-office-record/.

Galas, Marjorie. "For Award Consideration: Costume Designer Janie Bryant's Work in 'It.'" *LA411*. 11 Dec. 2017. https://www.la411.com/blog/post/it-costume-designer-janie-bryant-emmy-winning-costume-design.

Gompf, Michelle Leigh. "The Disturbing Appeal of Pennywise." *The Many Lives of IT: Essays on the Stephen King Horror Franchise*, edited by Ron Riekki. Jefferson, NC: McFarland, 2020, pp. 109–119.

Grant, Barry Keith. "Screams on Screen: Paradigms of Horror." *Thinking After Dark* (Special Issue: Welcome to the World of Horror Video Games), vol. 4, no. 6 (2010): 1–17.

Grebey, James. "IT Chapter Two Twists Comic Relief into Something Awful." *SyFy Wire*. 6 Sept. 2019. https://www.syfy.com/syfywire/it-chapter-two-twists-comic-relief-into-something-awful.

Green, Anna. "Why Do We Laugh When We're Scared?" *Mental Floss*. 16 Oct. 2015. https://www.mentalfloss.com/article/69830/why-do-we-laugh-when-were-scared.

Harris, Jake. "There's No Such Thing as an 'Elevated Horror' Movie." *Book and Film Globe*. 7 Oct. 2020. https://www.bookandfilmglobe.com/film/theres-no-such-thing-as-an-elevated-horror-movie/.

Heald, Helena. "What is Post-Horror? A Q&A with David Church, author of *Post-Horror: Art, Genre, and Cultural Elevation*." Edinburgh University Press. 29 Oct. 2021. https://www.euppublishingblog.com/2021/10/29/what-is-post-horror-a-qa-with-david-church-author-of-post-horror-art-genre-and-cultural-elevation/.

"It." *Box Office Mojo*. n.d. https://www.boxofficemojo.com/release/rl3481241089/.

IT. Directed by Tommy Lee Wallace. Performances by Tim Curry, Jonathan Brandis, Brandon Crane, Seth Green, Adam Faraizl, Ben Heller, Emily Perkins, Marlon Taylor, Richard Thomas, John Ritter, Harry Anderson, Dennis Christopher, Richard Masur, Annette O'Toole, and Tim Reid. ABC, 1990.

IT Chapter One. Directed by Andy Muschietti. Performances by Bill Skarsgård, Jaeden Martell, Wyatt Oleff, Jack Dylan Grazer, Finn Wolfhard. Sophia Lillis, Chosen Jacobs, and Jeremy Ray Taylor. Warner Bros., 2017.

"It Chapter Two." *Box Office Mojo*. n.d. https://www.boxofficemojo.com/release/rl1107461633/.

IT Chapter Two. Directed by Andy Muschietti. Performances by Bill Skarsgård, James McAvoy, Jessica Chastain, Bill Hader, Isaiah Mustafa, Jay Ryan, James Ransone, Andy Bean, Jaeden Martell, Wyatt Oleff, Jack Dylan Grazer, Finn Wolfhard. Sophia Lillis, Chosen Jacobs, and Jeremy Ray Taylor. Warner Bros., 2019.

Jaroudi, Iman. "Horrific Homophobia: Queer (Mis)Representation in Horror." *Broad Recognition*. 29 Oct. 2020. https://www.broadsatyale.com/queer-misrepresentation-in-horror/.

Kennedy, Michael. "IT: Everything We Know about the Director's Cut & Supercut." *Screen Rant*. 13 Dec. 2020. https://www.screenrant.com/it-movies-stephen-king-directors-cut-supercut-explained/.

King, Stephen. *Danse Macabre*. New York: Gallery Books, 2010 (1981).

———. *IT*. Viking, 1986.

———. "A Letter from Stephen." *StephenKing.com*. 2013. https://www.stephenking.com/promo/utd_on_tv/letter.html.

Knight, Jacob. "There's No Such Thing as an 'Elevated Horror Movie' (And Yes, 'Hereditary' is a Horror Movie)." *Slash Film*. 8 June 2018. https://www.slashfilm.com/elevated-horror/.

Kristeva, Julia. *Powers of Horror: An Essay on Abjection*, translated by Leon S. Roudiez. New York: Columbia University Press, 1980.

Leitch, Thomas. *Film Adaptation and Its Discontents: From* Gone with the Wind *to* The Passion of the Christ. Baltimore: Johns Hopkins University Press, 2007.

McAndrew, Frank T. "The Psychology Behind Why Clowns Creep Us Out." *The Conversation*. 28 Sept. 2016. https://www.theconversation.com/the-psychology-behind-why-clowns-creep-us- out-65936.

McRobbie, Linda Rodriguez. "The History and Psychology of Clowns Being Scary." *Smithsonian Magazine*. 31 July 2013. https://www.smithsonianmag.com/arts-culture/the-history-and-psychology-of-clowns-being-scary-20394516/.

Magistrale, Tony. *Landscape of Fear: Stephen King's American Gothic*. Madison: University of Wisconsin Press, 1988.

———. *Stephen King: The Second Decade*, Danse Macabre *to* The Dark Half. (Twayne's United States Authors Series). New York: Twayne, 1992.

Martin, Nick. "Native Spirituality is Not For Sale." *The New Republic*. 16 Sept. 2019. https://www.newrepublic.com/article/155010/it-chapter-two-great-american-tradition-selling-native-spirituality.

Metzger, Patrick. "The Nostalgia Pendulum: A Rolling 30-Year Cycle of Pop Culture Trends." *The Patterning*. 13 Feb. 2017. https://www.thepatterning.com/2017/02/13/the-nostalgia-pendulum-a-rolling-30-year-cycle-of-pop-culture-trends/.

Moon, Ra. "Where Was It Filmed? Stephen King's It Chapter 1 & 2 Filming Locations." *Atlas of Wonders*. 2020. https://www.atlasofwonders.com/2017/09/it-filming-locations.html.

Mulvey, Laura. "Visual Pleasure and Narrative Cinema." *Feminist Film Theory: A Reader*, edited by Sue Thornham. New York: New York University Press, 1999 (1975), pp. 58–69.

Nathan, Ian. *Stephen King at the Movies: A Complete History of the Film and Television Adaptations from the Master of Horror*. London: Palazzo, 2019.

Naughton, Keith and Bill Vlasic. "The Nostalgia Boom." *Business Week*, no. 3570 (1998): 58–64.

Nicholson, Tom. "The 2010s Were The Decade When Horror Got Smart." *Esquire*. 20 Dec. 2019. https://www.esquire.com/uk/culture/film/a30284121/elevated-horror-2010s-peele-eggers-aster-blumhouse/.

Nowell, Richard. *Blood Money: A History of the First Teen Slasher Cycle*. London: Bloomsbury, 2010.

Paz, Jordynn. "The Real Monster Wasn't the Clown, It was the Cultural Ignorance." *Montana Kaimin*. 27 Sept. 2019. https://www.montanakaimin.com/opinion/the-real-monster-wasnt-the-clown-it-was-the-cultural-ignorance/article_6cde5860-e170-11e9-9b7d-0707847a9f6c.html (this source cannot be accessed in the EEA or the UK).

Pfeifer, Theresa H. "Deconstructing Cartesian Dualisms of Western Racialized Systems: A Study in the Colors Black and White." *Journal of Black Studies*, vol. 39, no. 4 (2009): 528–547.

Pulliam, June. "'Best Not to Look Back': Monstrosity, Medium and Genre in Tommy Lee Wallace's It (1990)." *The Many Lives of IT: Essays on the Stephen King Horror Franchise*, edited by Ron Riekki. Jefferson, NC: McFarland, 2020, pp. 84–94.

Punter, David. *The Literature of Terror: A History of Gothic Fictions from 1765 to the Present Day, Vol. 1: The Gothic Tradition*, 2nd ed. Oxfordshire: Routledge, 1996.

Radford, Benjamin. *Bad Clowns*. Albuquerque: University of New Mexico Press, 2016.

Robinson, Tasha. "Stephen King's It is the Rare Monster Movie with Too Much Monster." *The Verge*. 6 Sept. 2017. https://www.theverge.com/2017/9/6/16257788/it-movie-review-stephen-king-andy-muschietti-pennywise-the-clown.

Romain, Lindsey. "6 Theories About The Kid, Bill Skarsgård's Creepy Character on 'Castle Rock.'" *Thrillist*. 17 Aug. 2018. https://www.thrillist.com/entertainment/nation/castle-rock-season-1-theories-who-is-the-kid-bill-skarsgard.

Romaneski, Peter Larkin. *The Gothic Place as the Center of Power and Ruin*. (Masters Thesis). Florida State University. 2009. https://www.diginole.lib.fsu.edu/islandora/object/fsu%3A176315.

Romano, Aja. "The Great Clown Panic of 2016 is a Hoax. But the Terrifying Side of Clowns is Real." *Vox.* 12 Oct. 2016. https://www.vox.com/culture/2016/10/12/13122196/clown-panic-hoax-history.

Schaefer, Sandy. "Stephen King's 'It' Getting Two-Film Adaptation by 'Jane Eyre' Director." *Screen Rant.* 8 June 2012. https://www.screenrant.com/stephen-king-it-movies-cary-fukunaga/.

Scott, A.O. "Review: 'It' Brings Back Stephen King's Killer Clown." *The New York Times.* 6 Sept. 2017. https://www.nytimes.com/2017/09/06/movies/it-review-stephen-king.html.

Sears, John. *Stephen King's Gothic.* (Gothic Literary Studies). Cardiff: University of Wales Press, 2011.

Shary, Timothy. *Generation Multiplex: The Image of Youth in American Cinema after 1980.* Austin: University of Texas Press, 2014.

Shetty, Karishma. "EXCLUSIVE: Stephen King on IT: Chapter 2: It's Not a Sequel; It's the Second Half of One Unified Story." *Pinkvilla.* 6 Sept. 2019. https://www.pinkvilla.com/entertainment/exclusives/exclusive-stephen-king-it-chapter-2-it-s-not-sequel-it-s-second-half-one-unified-story-471962.

Smith, Brian W. "The Clown Will Eat You Now." *The Many Lives of IT: Essays on the Stephen King Horror Franchise*, edited by Ron Riekki. Jefferson, NC: McFarland, 2020, pp. 181–187.

Smythe, James. "Fears of a Clown: Why the Original It Will Always Be the Best." *The Guardian.* 4 Sept. 2019. https://www.theguardian.com/tv-and-radio/2019/sep/04/it-clown-miniseries-tim-curry-stephen-king.

Southern Poverty Law Center. "The Year in Hate and Extremism 2019: A Report from the Southern Poverty Law Center." *Southern Poverty Law Center.* 2019. https://www.splcenter.org/sites/default/files/yih_2020_final.pdf.

"The Summer of IT—Chapter Two: IT Ends." *IT: Chapter Two.* Directed by Constantine Nasr. Rivendell Films, 2020.

Trumbore, Dave. "'It': Bill Skarsgård's Creepy New Pennywise Costume Revealed." *Collider.* 16 Aug. 2016. https://www.collider.com/it-movie-pennywise-costume-bill-skarsgard/.

Verevis, Constantine. *Film Remakes*. Edinburgh: Edinburgh University Press, 2005.

———. "Redefining the Sequel: The Case of the (Living) Dead." *Second Takes: Critical Approaches to the Film Sequel*, edited by Carolyn Jess-Cooke and Constantine Verevis. Albany: State University of New York Press, 2010, pp. 11–29.

Vincent, Bev. *The Stephen King Illustrated Companion: Manuscripts, Correspondence, Drawings, and Memorabilia from the Master of Modern Horror*. New York: Metro Books, 2009.

Walker, Tim. "What is Behind America's Hysterical Obsession with Creepy Clowns?" *Independent*. 6 Oct. 2016. https://www.independent.co.uk/news/world/americas/america-s-hysterical-obsession-creepy-clowns-a7349586.html.

Wampler, Scott. "You Might've Missed One of IT's Best Scares." *Birth. Movies. Death.* 10 Sept. 2017. https://www.birthmoviesdeath.com/2017/09/10/you-might-have-missed-one-of-its-best-scares.

Warren, Joey. "LGBTQ+ Representation in Horror." *The Current*. 11 Feb. 2020. https://www.thecurrentmsu.com/2020/02/12/lgbtq-representation-in-horror/.

Wax, Alyse. *The World of IT*. New York: Abrams, 2019.

Wigler, Josh. "'Castle Rock': How Hulu's Stephen King Anthology Series Was Born." *Hollywood Reporter*. 25 July 2018. https://www.hollywoodreporter.com/live-feed/castle-rock-series-premiere-stephen-king-hulu-series-explained-1129538.

Williams, Owen. "Stephen King's It – Everything You Need to Know." *Empire Online*. 11 Aug. 2016. https://www.empireonline.com/movies/features/stephen-king-everything-need-know/.

Wood, Robin. "An Introduction to the American Horror Film." *The Monster Theory Reader*, edited by Jeffrey Andrew Weinstock. Minneapolis: University of Minnesota Press, 2020 (1979), pp. 108–135.

www.ingramcontent.com/pod-product-compliance
Lightning Source LLC
Chambersburg PA
CBHW070403240426
43661CB00056B/2521